Horoscope
2022

· · · · · · · · · · · · · · · · ·

Pisces

20 February – 20 March

igloobooks

igloobooks

Published in 2021
First published in the UK by Igloo Books Ltd
An imprint of Igloo Books Ltd
Cottage Farm, NN6 0BJ, UK
Owned by Bonnier Books
Sveavägen 56, Stockholm, Sweden
www.igloobooks.com

0721 001
2 4 6 8 10 9 7 5 3 1
ISBN 978-1-80022-526-8

Written by Belinda Campbell and Denise Evans

Designed by Simon Parker
Edited by Natalie Graham

Printed and manufactured in China

CONTENTS
. . . .

INTRODUCTION
. . . .

This 15-month guide has been designed and written to give
a concise and accessible insight into both the nature of your
star sign and the year ahead. Divided into two main sections,
the first section of this guide will give you an overview of your
character in order to help you understand how you think,
perceive the world and interact with others and – perhaps just
as importantly – why. You'll soon see that your zodiac sign
is not just affected by a few stars in the sky, but by planets,
elements and a whole host of other factors, too.

The second section of this guide is made up of daily forecasts.
Use these to increase your awareness of what might appear on
your horizon so that you're better equipped to deal with the
days ahead. While this should never be used to dictate your
life, it can be useful to see how your energies might be affected
or influenced, which in turn can help you prepare for what life
might throw your way.

By the end of these 15 months, these two sections should
have given you a deeper understanding and awareness of
yourself and, in turn, the world around you. There are never
any definite certainties, but with an open mind you will find
guidance for what might be, and learn to take more control of
your own destiny.

THE CHARACTER OF THE TWO FISH

· · · · · · · · · · · · · · · · · · · ·

Compassionate, creative and charitable, Pisceans are the visionary dreamers who can breathe magic into the world. Whether it's their love of illusions like Derren Brown or their wonderful world building talents like Dr. Seuss, the enchanting Pisces can help bring joy and expand the minds of others. Neptune and Jupiter co-rule Pisces and provide this sign with a limitless imagination and a thirst for growth. At times, Pisceans can get lost in their fantasies and become detached from reality. A helping hand of support and encouragement from their friends and family might be needed to bring a lost Pisces back to reality. Wherever a Piscean's passion lies, however, their imagination will shine through, from Paul Hollywood's baking, to Michelangelo's Sistine Chapel and even to Albert Einstein's Theory of Relativity.

A Piscean's negative energy means that they can be more focused on their internal growth than on experiencing external stimulus. This means that mental, spiritual and emotional journeys are where this sign most likes to travel. The Two Fish that symbolise this sign can hint at a dual and slippery nature that makes this elusive siren of the sea hard to pin down. As a water sign that is governed by their emotions, they can get carried away on a fast-moving current and should be careful not to drown their loved ones in their, at times, overwhelming excitement. Belonging to the twelfth house in the zodiac calendar where sacrifice and devotion are key, there is surely no sign that is more generous with their time and love than pious Pisces. However, this sign should be careful that their self-sacrificing tendencies don't turn them into a martyr, as Pisceans can have a reputation for playing the victim at times.

As the snow begins to melt and the daffodils bloom, mutable Pisceans are born and bring with them a wise understanding of what has come before. Born at the end of winter and the end of the zodiac calendar, Pisces can be the most adaptable and understanding of all the signs, having learnt something from each of the star signs before them.

THE TWO FISH

Symbolised by the Two Fish, Pisces is one of the signs of the zodiac calendar with a dual symbol. The duality of Pisces could suggest flexibility in their emotions; getting excited for a project one day and bored the next may be all too familiar to many Pisceans. But being the last of the water signs, the Two Fish of Pisces can be capable of exploring the true depth and stretch of their emotions, encompassing both the allure of seductive Scorpio and sensitivity from family orientated Cancer. These slippery Fish can try and wriggle their way out of tight spots, coming up with the most fantastical of fibs. But if a reluctant Piscean constantly swims away from the truth, they may end up going in circles, chasing their own tales just as their symbol of the Two Fish are chasing each other's tails. This sign should try to remember that by accepting their slip-ups they can then learn from them and avoid making the same mistakes in the future.

JUPITER AND NEPTUNE

Co-ruled by the largest planet in the sky, Jupiter, and imaginative Neptune, Pisceans can certainly dream big. Jupiter, the ruler of the Gods in Roman mythology, ruled over the sky whilst his brother Neptune ruled the seas. This suggests that Pisceans can be a double force to be reckoned with. At times, dreamy Pisceans may have their heads stuck in their Jupiter clouds and at others they can feel as deeply as Neptune's waters and be as elusive and mythical as a mermaid. Jupiter is the fastest spinning planet in the solar system, resulting in it having the shortest days of all the planets, which a tardy Piscean might be quick to blame for their lateness. Pisceans can be incredibly understanding, but when pushed too far their anger can be as tempestuous as the sea of their co-ruler Neptune. Neptune is associated with spiritual intuition and its rule can help guide this compassionate water sign to better understand the world, whilst adventurous Jupiter can help them explore and find their place within it.

ELEMENTS, MODES AND POLARITIES

Each sign is made up of a unique combination of three defining groups: elements, modes and polarities. Each of these defining parts can manifest themselves in good and bad ways and none should be seen as a positive or a negative – including the polarities! Just like a jigsaw puzzle, piecing these groups together can help illuminate why each sign has certain characteristics and help us find a balance.

ELEMENTS

Fire: Dynamic and adventurous, signs with fire in them can be extroverted. Others are naturally drawn to them because of the positive light they give off, as well as their high levels of energy and confidence.

Earth: Signs with the earth element are steady and driven with their ambitions. They make for a solid friend, parent or partner due to their grounded influence and nurturing nature.

Air: The invisible element that influences each of the other elements significantly, air signs will provide much-needed perspective to others with their fair thinking, verbal skills and key ideas.

Water: Warm in the shallows and sometimes freezing as ice, this mysterious element is essential to the growth of everything around it, through its emotional depth and empathy

MODES

Cardinal: Pioneers of the calendar, cardinal signs jump-start each season and are the energetic go-getters.

Fixed: Marking the middle of the calendar, fixed signs firmly denote and value steadiness and reliability.

Mutable: As the seasons end, the mutable signs adapt and give themselves over gladly to the promise of change.

POLARITIES

Positive: Typically extroverted, positive signs take physical action and embrace outside stimulus in their life.

Negative: Usually introverted, negative signs value emotional development and experiencing life from the inside out.

PISCES IN BRIEF

The table below shows the key attributes of Pisceans.
Use it for quick reference and to understand more about this fascinating sign.

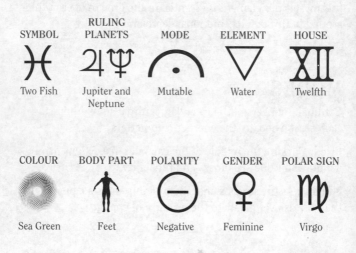

SYMBOL	RULING PLANETS	MODE	ELEMENT	HOUSE
Two Fish	Jupiter and Neptune	Mutable	Water	Twelfth

COLOUR	BODY PART	POLARITY	GENDER	POLAR SIGN
Sea Green	Feet	Negative	Feminine	Virgo

ROMANTIC RELATIONSHIPS

. . . .

Pisceans are the romantics of the zodiac and will no doubt fantasise about being swept off their feet, just like the starry-eyed characters from their favourite romance novels and films. Their intoxicating imagination and endless generosity rarely fail to charm so they are not likely to be short of admirers. As a mutable and self-sacrificing sign, overly generous Pisceans can be at risk of being too agreeable. Pisces should try not to just be the passenger in their relationships and instead take an active role in their love life. Sitting in the driving seat and taking on more responsibilities, whether it's choosing a restaurant for dinner or sorting out the home insurance, could boost an unsure Piscean's self-confidence and give their partner a needed break from always making the decisions.

As a mutable water sign, Pisceans can be adaptable to their partner's emotional needs and highly intuitive lovers. A Piscean's mutable quality means that they are also prone to the desire for change, which can have this sign flipping between their emotions and struggling to bind to just the one lover. Symbolised by not one but two fish makes Pisces a dual sign that is prone to going back and forth, changing their mind and their feelings. While the Two Fish are deciding on a partner who is best suited to them, they may have a few contenders in the running. This can hurt their potential partners if there is any deceit going on. If this sign can stick to the truth, then they should stand a better chance of staying out of hot water with their lovers. Under the philosophical influence of Jupiter and the spiritualism of Neptune, an easy-going Piscean might have a *que será, será* attitude when it comes to being with someone or not, and could be happy to leave it up to the universe to decide for them.

ARIES: COMPATIBILITY 2/5

Dreamy Pisces and action-loving Aries can learn a lot from each other. Watery Pisces can fear delving into the deep end of their desires and prefer to stay in the warmer, shallower waters of their comfort zone, generally choosing to emotionally support their partners' dreams over their own. Aries will want to help Pisces reach their full potential, but Aries should be wary of offending this water sign as Pisces is known to overflow with emotions when pushed. Pisces can offer much needed emotional support to Aries and the two can form a thoughtful connection deeper than most.

TAURUS: COMPATIBILITY 3/5

Taurus and Pisces are capable of having a highly sympathetic and understanding love. The practically minded Taurus should encourage the dreamy Pisces to live out their fantasies and work hard for themselves, not just others. In return, a Piscean will shower their Taurus in waves of love and gratitude for helping them realise their dreams. However, a Piscean would be wise not to saturate the relationship emotionally and spoil a Taurus. With Pisces being a water sign, Taureans can feel the nourishing effects this sign has in their earth element, and the life that these two can grow together is one well worth living.

GEMINI: COMPATIBILITY 3/5

As fluid as water and free-flowing as air, Pisces and Gemini can experience an extremely flexible and forgiving relationship when they fall for each other. Both mutable signs, this couple can be highly compatible and will not fight for leadership, but rather rule side by side. Whilst these two may not always perfectly understand each other, their open-minded attitudes will help resolve their disagreements. Whilst Gemini is led by the mind influence of Mercury, contrastingly, the Piscean's influence of water means that they can be ruled by their emotions. A meeting of the head and heart will be key.

CANCER: COMPATIBILITY 4 /5

These two feminine and water signs can be a vision of romance together. A Cancerian can truly identify with the changeable river of emotion that runs within Pisces, alternating speeds, directions and temperatures, because the same river runs within them too. Here are two signs that enjoy nurturing their loved ones, and so their love will be built on a mutual support system. Be mindful not to drown in the floods of emotions that both the Crab and Fish are capable of unleashing in their romantic relationships so that love and compassion can flow gently.

LEO: COMPATIBILITY 2/5

When Leo meets Pisces, each can bring out the best and worst in each other. Pisces can be a source of emotional encouragement for Leo, whilst Leo can help the dreamy Pisces take more action in their life. This allows them both to realise their dreams. Born in the twelfth house representing sacrifice, Pisces can be selfless whilst Leo, ruled by the Sun, can be the opposite. When these two sacrificing and self-serving characteristics are felt at their extremes, then things can quickly turn sour. However, mutable Pisces and fixed Leo can live in harmony if they both value each other's best qualities.

VIRGO: COMPATIBILITY 5/5

Opposites on the zodiac calendar, hands-on Virgo and mystical Pisces have a loving match but, like any couple, not without their struggles. The slippery Fish symbol of Pisces can hint at an elusiveness that can be attractive or frustrating to steady earth sign Virgo. Water and earth are elements that can create beautiful things together. However, in this couple the emotional Piscean and rational Virgo could be a tricky balancing act. These two are deep souls that can empathise and support one another probably better than any other signs and can happily and devotedly serve one another for endless days.

LIBRA: COMPATIBILITY 1/5

Whilst the enigmatic Pisces and suave Libra might be charmed by each other, theirs is a love that could struggle to reach fruition. Cardinal Libras are more likely to be the initiator in this relationship with mutable Pisceans, however, both signs can be struck with an inability to make decisions and this can leave them treading water; neither sinking nor swimming. Libras will be attracted to the artistic side of the creative Piscean and Pisceans are likely to flourish with the encouragement from their positive Libra partner. Finding a balance between Libra's extrovert and Piscean's introvert nature could allow their romance to bloom.

SCORPIO: COMPATIBILITY 4/5

Here are two water signs that will go to the ends of the Earth, or rather the depths of the oceans, for one another. Pisceans dream of finding that fantasy love and the enigmatic Scorpio can be just that for them, whilst the empathetic Pisces can be the kindred spirit that secretive Scorpios can finally be vulnerable with. A Piscean's mutable nature, which flows with change, can be at odds with the steadfast approach of a fixed Scorpio, but their differences mean that they have plenty to learn from each other. Emotional security and sensitivity are where these two thrive.

SAGITTARIUS: COMPATIBILITY 3/5

The roaming Sagittarius and the escapist Pisces could end up blissfully running off into the sunset together if they can learn from each other's differences. Both ruled by Jupiter, these two may indeed have been lucky to find one another. Jupiter gives Sagittarians and Pisceans a zest for life and their shared mutable modes will make their relationship open to continuous growth and change. Pisceans can lack the active side that many fire signs have whilst Sagittarians can lack compassion, which could clash with this sensitive water sign. By focusing on common interests, this deep pair could go far.

CAPRICORN: COMPATIBILITY 3/5

An earth and water love is bound to be a complimentary match, and the relationship between a Capricorn and Piscean may be about helping each other grow as individuals and flourish as a couple. Capricorn will bring a practical mind and an active spirit with their cardinal nature whilst the mutable Piscean will provide compassion and teach their Goat to be flexible. Both sides can retreat into themselves in times of great focus or reflection, particularly Pisceans if their Goat partner is being overbearing. However, their matching negative energies could form a deep emotional connection with each other and demonstrate true patience and dedication.

AQUARIUS: COMPATIBILITY 2/5

Two very giving signs such as Pisces and Aquarius could happily give themselves to each other in love. Whilst an air and water sign may struggle to understand one another, an Aquarian's intellect combined with the Piscean's compassion can form a relationship that speaks to both the heart and head if flexibility and patience is practised by the pair. A fixed and mutable combination can be a complimentary match, so long as Aquarians don't try to bend the will of their accommodating Piscean partner. The bond that these two can share when at its best can be sincere and spiritually liberating.

PISCES: COMPATIBILITY 2/5

Two Pisceans might easily capture each other's hearts and imaginations, but their easy-going mutable nature might make their feelings for one another struggle to gain traction and form a solid relationship. However, once these two, or four, Fish decide to commit, their love can be full of thoughtful gift giving and deep emotional understanding. These two water signs can be sponge-like with both positive and negative energies, so could bring out the best and worst in each other, depending on what they offer to the relationship, but at their shared core is a kind and patient soul.

FAMILY AND FRIENDS

· · · · · · · · · · · · · · · · · ·

As a water sign, Pisceans can be incredibly intuitive to the needs of their family and friends, attuned to picking up on even the slightest of changes in their loved one's emotions. A caring Piscean will not think twice about dropping what they are doing to go to a friend's aid, as is their self-sacrificing way. The kind words of a Piscean can help heal many emotional wounds, as they will often know just what to say, much to the relief of their family and friends. This eternally compassionate sign is only too glad to give themselves to others that need their support. Kindred spirits for Pisceans are the friends and family that reciprocate their support and encouragement. Fellow water sign Cancer could be a strong ally with their emotional sensitivity and cardinal go-getter attitude helping Pisceans make their dreams into a reality.

Whilst this sign is devoted to their family and friends, sticking to commitments can be a challenge for many slippery Pisceans. This sign should be wary of over-promising and consequently under-delivering in their eagerness to please and inability to say no. It may seem backwards to a Piscean that by saying 'no' they could strengthen the bonds that they cherish, however, their friends and family are far less likely to get angry if they say they cannot make a date straight away rather than flaking at the last minute. Time management is a skill that might not come naturally to this sign, but it is a tool that they should learn how to handle so that they can stay on top of their social calendar. Whilst writing and checking their appointments in a diary or calendar on their phone might not spark the imagination of a Pisces, it will make sure that they don't miss out on spending quality time with their loved ones.

FAMILY AND FRIENDS

Pisceans can be incredibly creative individuals, and this can be reflected in their enchanting homes. Their walls may be adorned with dreamy watercolour paintings or visitors might be greeted with aromas of burning incense to welcome them into a spiritual Piscean's home. A home by the sea or lake, where a Piscean can see their element of water regularly, may be where this sign decides to settle. Wherever a Pisces lives geographically, as a parent this sign can feel truly at home. The imaginative Pisces will want to fill their children's childhood with magic and wonder, making sure that Rudolph takes a bite from his carrot or leaving a coin and perhaps a tiny note from the Tooth Fairy. Pisceans, whilst not generally materialistic themselves, can be tempted to spoil their children and will always put their children's needs before their own, but they should be careful of giving or doing too much for them. Whether they are a parent, friend, cousin or sibling, a Piscean is ready to bring magic to the lives of others and emotionally support their loved ones.

MONEY AND CAREERS

....

Being a certain star sign will not dictate the type of career that you have, although the characteristics that fall under each sign could help you identify the areas in which you could potentially thrive. To succeed in the workplace, it is just as important to understand what you are good at as it is to know what you are less brilliant at, so that you can see the areas in which you will need to perhaps work harder in to achieve your career and financial goals.

Whilst Pisceans can have fantastic dreams about what careers they would like to have, they can lack the drive to make their fantasies a reality. A Piscean can get so blissfully lost in thinking about their dream job that they fail to take the necessary steps to reach their goals, especially if they are in the habit of underestimating themselves, but building their self-confidence usually helps them to take action. A compatible career path for Pisceans would be something that sparks their imagination and gets their creative juices flowing. Whether it's the music of Rihanna or the paintings of Renoir, a creative Piscean could look to aspirational figures that inspire them to turn their passion into a paid career. Another professional path that Pisces may prefer to follow is one where they can dedicate their time and energy towards improving the lives of others. Born in the twelfth house, which signifies service and sacrifice, Pisces can be some of the kindest and most generous of souls, so a caring career as a nurse, aid worker or foster parent could be best suited to the giving Pisces.

MONEY AND CAREERS

. . . .

When it comes to a Piscean's finances, money can trickle through their fingers as quickly as their element water does. This sign will not hesitate to buy something that catches their fancy, which can start to be an issue when they unwittingly spend beyond their means. The creative Piscean may have unsteady income, and not have much of a grip on their finances and the all-too-real world of budgets. If the mere thought of spreadsheets is bringing a Piscean out in hives, they would do well to pay for someone else to help with their expenses, particularly if they are self-employed. Earth signs like Taurus, Virgo, and Capricorn will usually have a flair for material things and their practical approach could help a disorganised Pisces handle their money more frugally, helping them establish boundaries to manage their incomings and outgoings. Whilst trusting Pisceans may be tempted to believe in a magical fix to their financial worries, they should avoid any get-rich-quick type schemes, as if it sounds too good to be true, it probably is.

Whilst you can't always choose who you work with, it can be advantageous to learn about colleagues' key characteristics through their star signs to try and work out the best ways of working with them. As a water sign, Pisceans can be swept up in negative and positive energies from their colleagues, so it's important for this sign to surround themselves with the latter and guard themselves against the former. Pisceans truly thrive on positive encouragement, so their neighbouring sign of Aquarius could be the optimistic and creative influence that helps a Piscean to reach their career dreams.

HEALTH AND WELLBEING

. . . .

Pisceans can be the ultimate escapism artists, living in their own fantasy and choosing to be blind to any painful issues in their real life. But even with lucky Jupiter co-ruling this sign, their problems won't often magically fix themselves. If a Piscean feels themselves drifting into escapism, bingeing on films or playing video games at all hours, then they may need to make a strong conscious effort to come back to reality. Whilst this sign may be tempted to blame others for their upset state, they could also be a victim of their own making. Pisceans feel deeply, and as a negative sign can internalise their distress. As a sensitive water sign, learning to let go of any emotional pain from the past and focusing on the positives of the present will do wonders for their wellbeing. Practising mindfulness through meditation can be a useful tool for a spiritual Piscean to ease their anxieties and bring them back to a present state of calm.

Self-love is important for every sign, but Pisceans can easily forget to nurture themselves while they are busy looking after everyone else. Taking time to indulge their creative side can be essential to a Piscean's happiness, but is something they sometimes sacrifice for the sake of others. If a Piscean has an artistic talent, be it with words, art, music, food or anything else, they should indulge in their creativity and enjoy the healing magic that they can create. Taking time for themselves may have the consequence of having less time for others, which can feel selfish to this giving sign, but taking even an hour to enjoy a bath, read a book or hone their chosen art is vital for this sign's health and wellbeing. Once a depleted Piscean has been able to recharge their batteries, they will almost certainly find that they are able to give much more of themselves to the world as a direct result.

Physical activity is a key way for everyone to stay fit, no matter their star sign, but Pisceans can be more interested in stretching their imagination than they are their bodies. If Pisces wants to get into a good exercise routine, finding a sport or physical activity that they enjoy and can be creative in will be important. As a water sign, Pisces could quite literally be in their element whilst swimming, surfing or ice skating. If water or an ice rink aren't readily accessible to this sign, their associated body part, feet, could have them dancing their way to fitness in a Zumba class or at their favourite music club. Pisceans will no doubt appreciate the creativity of music and dance, and getting healthier will just be a happy bonus for them. Whilst it might be tempting for a Pisces to stick on their best heels before hitting the dance floor, wearing comfier footwear could save them some plasters and keep their associated body part happy and healthy.

Pisces

....

DAILY FORECASTS
for 2021

OCTOBER

Friday 1st

Mercury retrograde challenges Pluto today. You may see some unsavoury activity within your friendship groups. It's likely to be secretive, or possibly even nasty and malicious, causing a rift within the group. Your inclination is to join in and make your point. You could be the peacemaker now if you choose.

Saturday 2nd

Tensions are still high but there's a slim chance you may be able to withdraw from it all. Venus helps to make any losses or permanent changes in your social circle a little easier. You might find that they're not such a big loss after all.

Sunday 3rd

As the Moon enters your relationship sector, you may desire to spend time with a partner who exudes common sense and virtuousness. They could help you to see the bigger picture and details you might have missed. Time alone to process your thoughts will also be of value to you later today.

Monday 4th

Expect the unexpected. This may come in the form of a surprise from your partner in an attempt to cheer you up. You've lost sight of your inner compass, but this is fine. There's no point dwelling on possibilities when there's more urgent work to be done.

Tuesday 5th

Pluto and Venus once again make good contacts to the Moon. This means that you can make changes or deal with judgements with a little more compassion. This afternoon your sense of fairness makes a decision easier. Emotions can be put aside, and you can use logic and reason.

Wednesday 6th

A new moon meets Mars and Mercury retrograde in your intimacy sector. This can be quite intense as Pluto turns direct too. Something has permanently ended and here's the new start you've been waiting for. Just don't sign any commitments yet. Actions begun after the retrograde are more likely to stick.

Thursday 7th

Venus enters your career sector. She'll show you the joy of bringing harmony and optimism to the workplace. You may turn inwards now and do some introspection. Plant seeds of ideas to enhance your knowledge of deep and philosophical thought. Spiritual matters attract you now.

Friday 8th

The Sun meets Mars today. This is a powerhouse of energy for you to access and use in your intimate sector. You might see this as confirmation of the goals you set at new moon. An intense Moon stirs something up inside you and you may wish to share this with someone close.

Saturday 9th

Mercury meets Mars and the Sun. Be very careful as your mental faculties may be foggy or too rash. There's also the chance of accidents or burn-out now. Feminine intuition is strong today. Pay attention and you may produce miracles.

Sunday 10th

Saturn turns direct. This is good news if you've been paying attention to his lessons. He will relax his grip on you and your hidden sector will experience a heavy weight being lifted from it. A green light tells you to make haste and get on with a new project.

Monday 11th

You may sense some hesitation within your wider friendship groups. The truth has come out and you could see false friends drop away. Teachers and leaders may expose themselves as fake. Maybe it's just you awakening to a new level of awareness. Think about it.

Tuesday 12th

There may be a further shift or a bright idea forming in your mind. It's possible that you're thinking in another way and wish to share this with a friend or group. Don't be shy, people welcome your ideas and will appreciate that you've participated in the group.

Wednesday 13th

Today's a lucky day as you see something of your true north, but this time you're seeing it with a responsible, disciplined mind. You may have disregarded pie-in-the-sky ideas and have now come around to basing your plans on thoroughly grounded, practical concepts.

Thursday 14th

The Moon meets newly direct Saturn in your hidden sector. Consider this as a call to the headmaster's office. You'll get a full report of your activities this year. He will tell you if you've passed the test. Other planetary aspects are favourable. You may be pleased with yourself.

Friday 15th

Both Sun and Moon connect to your ruler. Jupiter's famous luck-bringing qualities are available to you, but not in a direct way. Open your mind and take on board any subtle messages you receive. Jupiter strokes your ego and hits an emotional trigger, to which you will need to react.

Saturday 16th

Today you may take an overdue rest and allow yourself some downtime. The Moon in your sign makes you pause and reflect on the past and future. You may feel challenged, but you could also take this opportunity to bring old skills back into use for your future goals and aspirations.

Sunday 17th

Your ruler turns direct. Mark what happens that can enhance your growth and let you reach out to the wider world. The Moon sits with Neptune, so you might get a good idea of how this will pan out for you. This energy is too good to ignore. Use it or lose it.

Monday 18th

Mercury also turns direct. You may feel light as a feather and choose to enjoy some free time doing nothing much. Look around you and evaluate your possessions and what they mean to you. You might declutter and feel even freer. This would be a worthwhile activity.

Tuesday 19th

The Moon is challenged by newly direct Mercury. You are asked to look at what may need to be rectified to give you peace of mind. Money matters need attention. Look at subscriptions which may no longer be active. Investments you share with another might be accessed.

Wednesday 20th

A full moon in your finance and values sector confirms that you need to look at your bank balance. It's possible that you've overspent or missed important payments. However, the opposite is also true, and you may have increased your balance.

Thursday 21st

Watch your temper today. Saturn and Uranus are making it difficult for you to hold your tongue and you don't want to undo all the good work you've done this year. Play by the rules and if someone is provoking you, bid them farewell. Enjoy a little luxury today if you can.

Friday 22nd

Mars and Pluto are squaring off and you may see more arguments within your social sector. This may change the way you put energy into groups as you realise that they're not in line with your best interests. You may have an emotional reaction to something you thought you had dealt with.

Saturday 23rd

The Sun enters your travel sector. Prepare to be enlightened about subjects you've previously thought nothing of. This may be a time where you change and develop your ideas about other cultures and wish to discover more about religion, philosophy or subjects such as astrology and psychology. Enjoy some family fun this weekend.

Sunday 24th

Talk to your nearest and dearest about your role in the family and at work. You may receive some good advice from siblings. Help is available if you need to balance your home and work duties. You may enjoy both areas a lot more if you slim down your responsibilities.

Monday 25th

It may be futile to get back on your personal path today as other issues demand your attention. There's much joy to be had from working on your personal issues as Jupiter is now in the position to help you move along quickly. You receive courage and energy from Mars to enter unknown territory.

Tuesday 26th

Work duties might exhaust you and take you far away from your goals. This may make you extra sensitive. You desire to be creative or pursue your love interests, but find that there's no time left in the day, which could upset you.

Wednesday 27th

Your heart and mind may feel separated. Your default is to go with your heart, and you could find that you're drifting off into fantasy land or ignoring your practical responsibilities. This is a frustrating time for you. You will need to be adaptable and go with the flow.

Thursday 28th

Stand up for yourself. Don't let yourself be dragged into other people's dramas. You may be called upon to mediate a situation, but this isn't your job and it may drain more energy than you can spare right now. Send love to those suffering, but opt out of being the one to fix them if you need to.

Friday 29th

You have the gift of the gab and can persuade people to do anything. Be mindful of your conversations, as there's a possibility that you engage in a discussion which others aren't ready to hear. You may shock someone with your outspokenness.

Saturday 30th

Today you may yearn for time with a partner. You want some time where you are cared for or even seduced. Mars moving into your travel sector opens up avenues for exploring the dark and mysterious sides of life. You need a travel guide and your partner is offering their services.

Sunday 31st

Allow yourself some quality time with someone you love and admire. They may have a way of solving problems which hasn't occurred to you. You might find that you have mutual regard for each other's views today and you can be a force of strength when together.

NOVEMBER

· · · · · · · · · · · · · · · · · · ·

Monday 1st

The pace is picking up now. There could be issues regarding money that need your attention. This may involve a partner or group of people. You have a good sense of responsibility and your major chores get done easily. Don't worry if you have no time to dream. Today is for practical matters.

Tuesday 2nd

Mercury and Pluto are at odds today. You may have difficult conversations with someone or bring something to a permanent end. Saturn graces you with the tact needed to approach this and come to the best possible outcome for all. This will free up some mental space.

Wednesday 3rd

You may be having second thoughts or regrets. The Moon and Mercury meet up and you could experience turmoil. Overthinking is possible and this will have an emotional effect. Just be fair; there's not much more you can do. Don't stress about things you can't control.

Thursday 4th

There's a new moon in your travel sector. This may set you on a path of deep discovery via long-distance vacations or higher education courses. This Moon makes some touchy connections and will possibly stir up something you now need to deal with once and for all.

Friday 5th

The Sun opposes Uranus and affects your style of conversation. You may hear or speak some shocking words. Venus and Mercury both change signs and you might feel the shift as a desire to connect with people outside your normal circle. Your mind is extra inquisitive now. What do you desire to know?

Saturday 6th

The energy today suggests that you're swimming into unknown waters and looking around. New friends could come along just in time for the festive season. Keep your eyes and ears open for anything that's seductive or exotic. You may decide on dining out this evening to satisfy that craving.

Sunday 7th

The Moon connects to both of your rulers. Neptune is evasive and not showing your personal quest which means that Jupiter is getting all your attention in your hidden sector. You might not even notice what important inner work you achieve today, but it will be big.

Monday 8th

The Moon meets Venus and the energy is feminine and intuitive. This may affect your wider friendship groups or your social status at work. Other aspects suggest that you're willing to go the extra mile and make something happen today. It's possible that you're planning a social event.

Tuesday 9th

Be very careful as you may feel manipulated or controlled. Alternatively, it's you who is fully in control. The emotional Moon meets Pluto so this could go two ways. Neptune seduces you and you might take a step or two to realign yourself with your personal quest.

Wednesday 10th

The planetary energy is volatile, so watch your step. You may experience arguments, personal attacks or a complete change of mind from someone close or in authority. You will probably not escape any of this, so do your best to stay calm, kind and respectful.

Thursday 11th

Any tension today will be magnified by the Moon meeting Jupiter. There may be many triggers, which will test you beyond your comfort zone. You will need to assess whether the best option is to submit or stand up for yourself. Do what's right for you and gives you the least stress.

Friday 12th

The Moon dips into your sign and you may feel more like your usual self. This is a good time to pause and do nothing as you might not be sure how to move next. Take some time out and connect with your wider groups. Online associates could give you the distraction you require.

Saturday 13th

Breathe deeply and let it out. You've found your inner compass
again and feel back on track. Mars and Mercury offer you the
energy and mind to learn something that will benefit you.
However, Uranus sits opposite, so mind how you proceed as it
may have unexpected results.

Sunday 14th

Use today to check that your finances are healthy. You may
wish to invest or claim back money from a long-standing fund.
Overspending is also possible now, but you feel justified and
deserve it. Big plans for the season are being made and you
may be the coordinator.

Monday 15th

Someone may not be playing nicely in your social sector. A rift
between friends is likely. Disharmony amongst your friends or
work colleagues makes things awkward today. This doesn't sit
right with you. Do the responsible thing and your conscience
will be clear.

Tuesday 16th

There are important changes going on. This could also be
passive-aggressive or secretive behaviour. It may provoke your
sense of justice and you wish to sort it out. You might try to
step in and mediate. Step back, as there's a chance it isn't
your business.

Wednesday 17th

Mars opposes Uranus and this almost definitely means that you experience conflict. Conversations by mouth, email or messaging may get messy. This could also involve money, relationships or joint investments such as taxes, inheritance or other shared responsibilities. Don't sleep on it; sort it out before it becomes too stressful for all parties.

Thursday 18th

The tension continues. Mercury tries to help by giving you the power to speak and offer other perspectives. However, you're dealing with personalities that are stubborn and resistant to any peace offerings. This will be a tough day; hang in there and try to stay afloat.

Friday 19th

The full moon in your communications sector brings recent matters to a head. You may find an obvious solution now or decide to draw a line and let things go. You simply want the peace restored and may compromise your principles to achieve this. Rely on family this evening.

Saturday 20th

You just can't please everyone all the time. It's commendable that you try hard to do this, but you may have to accept defeat. Later you may look back and realise that this was the best possible move to make. Others will need to own their roles in this upset and move on.

Sunday 21st

Spending time with your family will bring you pleasure today. Light-hearted chatter may be a relief after the recent tension you have had. Neptune is hiding from you and you perceive this as a challenge. If you can discuss future plans with family then do so, but if they don't understand, don't take it personally.

Monday 22nd

The Sun moves into your career sector. This will have the effect of making you investigate enhancing your work prospects and possibly travelling. There may be a way of combining both. This is a good day for romance as Venus and Mars are connecting well.

Tuesday 23rd

Be creative today. There's a wash of watery energy available for you to wallow in. Romance, art, music and spiritual matters are all highlighted for you. You may have to choose between being a nurturer or a lover today, but this is all part of your adaptable nature.

Wednesday 24th

Mercury enters your career sector. Maybe this is the time to ask for a raise or a different, more research-based role. You may be feeling sensitive and protective of what you value. It's possible that a new romance or art project isn't ready to be announced to the world.

Thursday 25th

Today you may do your own thing in your own way and ignore consequences. You're feeling braver now and have something you would like to show off to the world. Venus and Mars are connecting well, so this is likely to be something that you're very passionate about.

Friday 26th

What you want for yourself and what you want for the wider world is at odds today. You're torn between making a selfish move and one that benefits the wider group. You do so much for others, you deserve this moment. Don't feel guilty about it.

Saturday 27th

The Moon moves into your relationship sector, but you may be hesitant to make any moves with a special person. You're afraid of saying the wrong thing or going too fast. It may be a better idea to quietly withdraw until you're sure this is what you want.

Sunday 28th

Your nerves are tingling, and you're alert to the possibility of something strange and new coming your way. This excites you but pulls you off course. The Moon opposes Neptune and you may be led astray by fantasies or false promises. Get a reality check today; ensure you know what you're doing.

Monday 29th

Mercury is in the heart of the Sun and is silent. At this time, you must switch on your intuition and listen for subtle messages. You're feeling positive and uplifted, so this shouldn't be too difficult for you. The energy is looking good, which comes as a relief after uncertainty.

Tuesday 30th

You aim for harmony today. Many of the planets combine to help you reconcile your inner and outer worlds. Deep feelings are surfacing now, and you may experience the return of old habits. Venus and Neptune make this a dreamy, romantic day, so make the most of it.

DECEMBER

· · · · · · · · · · · · · · · · · ·

Wednesday 1st

Neptune turns direct. This is great news for you as you're now free to forge ahead and go after what you deserve. Prepare to swim in deep waters and connect with your true north. As your co-ruler, Neptune will let you explore and guide you to do your best work now.

Thursday 2nd

An intense Moon helps you to take the first brave steps you need to walk your own path. Choose your guides and helpers wisely. Don't be reckless. Uranus is disturbing the ground you stand on and you may experience shifts in your psyche that confirm you're on your way.

Friday 3rd

The Moon meets hot-headed Mars. Your passions are foremost in your heart. Jupiter is opening and expanding your mind but go slowly as this may be overwhelming. There is still the day to day work to do so don't neglect it. Your journey will accommodate all parts of your life.

Saturday 4th

There is a new moon in your career sector. This will act as a starting point work wise. Perhaps there's a way that you can switch up your career goals and incorporate them into your new journey. This Moon meets Mercury, so take the time to research and explore possibilities.

Sunday 5th

Today you're determined and responsible. You enjoy some time with friends, but have the good sense not to overdo things. Enthusiasm and optimism make all that you do today a joy. People may try to knock you off your happy place, but the good energy is too strong. Be sensitive, but enjoy the good times.

Monday 6th

Mars and Pluto connect to tear down old structures that are holding you back. This may feel uncomfortable at first, but you might soon realise the benefits. Things will continue to shift as you adjust. Stay adaptable and this will be easy for you.

Tuesday 7th

The Moon meets Pluto and you feel an emotional pull to what has been released. Grieve this loss for the value it once held for you. Give gratitude for the space it has now made. This afternoon your altruistic side makes you reach out to a good cause, as if to celebrate.

Wednesday 8th

You may come across authority figures or leaders who attempt to pull you back into line. That is their line, not yours. You might need to be firm and politely decline their misguided but well-meaning advice. Remember that personal boundaries need to be healthy and strong.

Thursday 9th

Talking to new friends or acquaintances may help to confirm your new choices. You may have a moment of doubt and feel a little stuck. This is just a passing phase so relax and if need be, take some time alone with your thoughts if friends confuse you even more.

Friday 10th

The Moon is in your sign now and gives you some peace. You can use this time to get back in touch with your body or spirituality. Yoga, meditation or walking in nature may help. Little things will excite you as you feel your way on your journey.

Saturday 11th

Venus and Pluto meet up. This can herald a tricky situation where you may feel manipulated or controlled. You might not know how to react. As the Moon meets Neptune you're advised to be patient and maybe look at things from a different perspective. Don't be tempted to act just yet.

Sunday 12th

You may be itching to do something that you feel validates your choices and path. However, the planetary energy suggests that you need more time to evaluate the world around you as you're looking at it through different eyes now. The time for action will come soon.

Monday 13th

Mars moves into your career sector and Mercury into your social sector. As the festive season fast approaches, this may simply mean that social engagements and work deadlines are coming in. Alternatively, this can also mean that you network far and wide. Researching a new interest is always a good idea before acting.

Tuesday 14th

Today you're practical and methodical in all that you do. You can feel that things are going too slow but at the end of the day, you will see that you did your work well. You may feel you have to decline a social engagement and do overtime to meet deadlines. Don't be taken advantage of.

Wednesday 15th

You may be a bit sensitive today as you have no time to dream or study your personal interests. The Moon meets Uranus and your mood could be close to erupting into tears. This could also be burnout, so slow down, breathe and believe in yourself.

Thursday 16th

You're being advised to look after number one today. You may be feeling the pressure of trying to forge your own path and being coerced by others to join in some fun. This might not be to your taste right now if you prefer to lie low with family. Polite refusals may be needed.

Friday 17th

The Moon sits opposite Mars. This may mean that you see issues or conflicts arise between people of different genders. You could also have difficulty balancing both your work and family duties now. Something has to give; choose what is best for you alone.

Saturday 18th

You feel cast adrift as you try to realign yourself. Don't worry, Neptune hasn't abandoned you; there are simply other more pressing things to think about today. Enjoy a time of family chores and visits, which will make the festive time special. They're counting on you to be part of it.

Sunday 19th

A full moon occurs in your family sector and shows you the full scope of your achievements with your kin this year. Venus also turns retrograde. You may see the return of an old lover, a breakup or troubling relationships with women now.

Monday 20th

Your creative and romantic urges come out. You'll need to factor in some time to be with a lover or get musical, poetic or artistic. This will come easily and you will find your muse. This Moon opposes Mercury so things may be unclear at first, but soon there will be no stopping you.

Tuesday 21st

The winter solstice arrives and gives you an opportunity to pause and reflect before the mayhem happens. Give gratitude for the lessons you've learned this year. You may find that you are humble and more accepting of differences within the family at this time.

Wednesday 22nd

Today you're on top form. There's a lot of preparation to do and duties to perform. You love to serve others and today you do this with extra cheer. However, an elder in the family or your wider interest groups may have something to say to derail you.

Thursday 23rd

Your ruler Jupiter returns to the very last part of your chart. He's at the end of your hidden sector and asks that you check in with your deepest self today. Is there something that you've forgotten about or put to one side? Maybe the seasonal duties have caused you to neglect something important.

Friday 24th

Tension and arguments are possible today. The Moon is in your relationship sector but connects to planets which can be volatile. Be careful out there as you may witness accidents and mishaps. Slow down and double-check everything. Get your partner to help with the details.

Saturday 25th

Venus retrograde has returned to Pluto's arms. You may experience this as unfinished business with a current or past lover. This could come as a passing comment that acts as a trigger. Uranus and Mercury help to make this a day full of surprises and laughter, so don't dwell on the negative.

Sunday 26th

Time spent with a lover may give you both food for thought.
You might have fond memories return to you. Sharing
your dreams and visions with someone who is practical
and dependable may help you to begin grounding them in
reality.

Monday 27th

You should be able to enjoy a quiet day as the Moon is in
your intimacy sector and aims for harmony. It's possible
that something from your hidden sector comes up to
be healed, but this doesn't bother you and is perhaps a
welcome insight into past behaviours. You're outgoing and
personable today.

Tuesday 28th

Today you may experience something that rocks your happy
boat. Be careful who you share things with, as there could be
secrets and jealousy around you. The darker side of life rears
its head this evening. You might need to take cover. This will
need investigating, but maybe not today.

Wednesday 29th

Jupiter, your ruler, enters your sign. This is great news as he
will stay for a year and enhance everything he touches. You
will receive many blessings from the jolly planet, who can
enhance your joy, optimism and sense of adventure now. You
will reach out far and wide over the next year.

Thursday 30th

Mercury meets Pluto. He's receiving his new mission to take forward into 2022. All will be revealed soon. You may have a secret rendezvous today, as Venus retrograde is currently connecting to a seductive Moon. Be safe and remember your personal boundaries.

Friday 31st

As the Moon meets Mars in your career sector, you get a boost of confidence about your work. You may be more driven to succeed in the new year. Your motivation can be high, and you're eager to get back into a routine. But first, enjoy any celebrations you participate in tonight.

Pisces

....

DAILY FORECASTS
for 2022

JANUARY

. . . .

Saturday 1st

Happy New Year and welcome to 2022. While you are enjoying some free time, make sure that there is nothing you have neglected regarding your social groups. You may have to tie up loose ends now before a new cycle begins. Connect with important people before you get busy again.

Sunday 2nd

A new moon gives you the chance to set intentions, which may concern your work goals. An action plan may be put in place ready for the long climb up the corporate ladder this year. Your mind could be full of ideas and may even keep you awake at night. Jot things down, then get some rest.

Monday 3rd

You may have noticed a return of someone from your past recently. This may have caused some control issues. If this was an old lover, you may find that it has unsettled you and you think a lot about this today. Let the past stay in the past. Don't be too soft and have faith in your own perceptions.

Tuesday 4th

A busy mind will affect your mood and you may be struggling to concentrate on daily routines. Restless energy upsets you, as you aren't sure what to do with it. You wish to do the right thing, but can't see what that is right now. Discussing it is no help today, so let the matter rest on the backburner.

Wednesday 5th

You may have a stronger than average need to reach out or expand your horizons. This may go hand-in-hand with your wish to escape something from the past or to put something well behind you. Put your energy into breaking free in some way, even if it scares you.

Thursday 6th

An optimistic day awaits you and you may find that others are attracted to your mood. A spring in your step is a tell-tale sign that you have something you need to communicate, but for now, it's staying secret. Try making a vision board for the year.

Friday 7th

That ghost from the past isn't bothering you today. You may have filed it away or dealt with it in a kindly manner. Instead, you seem to connect to your life purpose and your inner compass is aligned and showing you the way forward. You understand the need for a new you.

Saturday 8th

Today you may take time to look at what you have around you and evaluate the worth of it all. This could mean that you spend the day decluttering and making everything fresh. A clean environment and a healthy bank balance are the best way to start the year.

· · · · · · · · · · · · · · · · · ·

Sunday 9th

Be mindful of who you are in contact with today. You may experience ego clashes or subtle manipulation, which can leave you confused. Social groups may not be as helpful as you wish. This may be something that only you can sort out. It's best done this evening when you have more energy.

Monday 10th

Restriction may arise within your friendship groups and you may see a need for change or loss in this area. Conversations with the right people will help you to understand what you are feeling. Siblings and childhood friends are supportive as you need to process feelings with someone you trust.

Tuesday 11th

Today can be somewhat frustrating and you risk losing your patience and blowing a fuse. Keep tricky conversations to a minimum. Try to be realistic and remember that not everyone is as sensitive as you. Don't take things personally if you feel like you are being attacked.

Wednesday 12th

Self-control is an issue today, but you manage to muster enough to get you through a tricky situation. You may feel more grounded than usual and this helps you to see a situation for what it is. Emotional choices and decisions don't come into it, as today you're thinking in a practical way.

Thursday 13th

Mercury turns retrograde tomorrow, so use today to back up devices and double-check travel plans. Family matters need your attention and you may need to step up and be the responsible one. Alternatively, they may look to you for some optimism and cheering up. Give what you can.

Friday 14th

Your thought processes may be muddled or multi-layered now with Mercury retrograde. Now, it's very important that you note everything and work on it another time. You may have to put down rules and regulations within your family group. A sense of duty and leadership is strong for you.

Saturday 15th

Today can be very tiring and you may need to set limits on how much you do for others. Use the weekend time to do what feeds your soul and fills your own cup. This may be intimate, romantic time, creative pursuits or cooking with a loved one.

Sunday 16th

Matters of the heart may bother you today as you may need to transform or reject an offer of love or friendship. You will need to think this through in peace and try to be as objective as you can. If it doesn't align with your soul's purpose, let it go.

Monday 17th

You wish to stay cosy and protected doing what you love. However, a full moon in your love and romance arena may show a completion or ending that upsets you. You may be too sensitive and emotional to work this out rationally. Stay on track and hold on to your own agenda.

Tuesday 18th

Uranus turns direct today, which can be helpful if you need to have difficult conversations. You may be able to assert yourself more than usual and stand up for what you believe in. Check-in with your health today and ensure that you have the emotional strength to deal with problems.

Wednesday 19th

Today can be difficult as you may struggle with your conscience and wonder if you have done the right thing. This feeling will pass and after some thought, you will be sure that you are on the right path. Always act responsibly and with respect, especially for yourself.

Thursday 20th

You may wish to consult a close partner today, as they may be more practical and methodical when dealing with tricky situations. Your energy levels pick up and you may adopt an attitude whereby you get on with the job in hand and put your emotions aside. Prioritise what you can do.

Friday 21st

There is a lot of earthy, grounding energy for you to access today. Conversations will be straight forward, although you may need to have tactic talks within your social groups. Someone may not be very pleased by this, but it's the right thing to do and will ultimately benefit all.

Saturday 22nd

You may wake feeling at odds with your inner compass and try to put it right. This may be by making a permanent ending to make space for something new. Take time to evaluate your social and interest groups for their worth in your life.

Sunday 23rd

Listen very carefully to what your subconscious is bringing up. Intuition is high today. You may feel an urge to act or a worry about unfinished business. Leave it for today and let yourself have some downtime. If your thought processes want to do overtime, let them. Now is not the time to speak or act.

Monday 24th

Mars boosts your social groups and there may be something you suddenly wish to join. Getting active or adding your name to social issues may be good for you. Don't be put off by second thoughts this evening; this is likely to be you overthinking and being too sensitive about doing the right thing.

Tuesday 25th

This is a busy day as your emotions may jump back and forth. You desire to seek new pastures and have more adventures. These may include foreign travel or higher education, and are likely to be a little different to the norm. You may find it difficult to stay on track.

Wednesday 26th

Mercury retrogrades back into your friendship sector. You may be reassessing your role in groups and thinking about how you can take on other duties that are more fulfilling. There may be a calling here, but you will need to do all the background research before committing.

Thursday 27th

There is a chance that you may bring back skills learned in the past. These may help to secure a better position in the workplace. The old you may help the new you in ways you never thought possible. Don't blow your own trumpet though; let it quietly toot and be heard.

Friday 28th

Your sense of duty may distract you from aligning with your inner compass, but there is a reason for this. You may have soul work that requires your attention or other obligations that you can't get out of. Nevertheless, acting responsibly will be the right thing to do today.

Saturday 29th

If you listen very carefully to messages or signs, you may get a new mission today. Consider it and leave it on file for now. Venus turns direct, meaning that any troubles in love or friendships may be eased. Time with friends this evening can be lively and enjoyable.

Sunday 30th

You may have an emotional pull towards something you thought you had let go. Alternatively, you may be at peace now with a troublesome acquaintance. Don't let offhand and careless remarks spoil the remainder of your weekend. Instead, discuss your dreams with like-minded friends and share your hopes for the future.

Monday 31st

You may have a sleepless night and wake feeling determined
to start a new mission. Hold that thought. Wait until you are
certain and have done all the necessary research. Make time
for introspection this evening and look at how this mission
will fit into your need to change the world.

FEBRUARY
· · · · · · · · · · · · · · · · · ·

Tuesday 1st
A new moon helps you to think about the goals you wish
to set regarding self-improvement. You may find that there
are conflicts between what you want for yourself and your
obligations to your family. Be responsible and set limits or new
boundaries. You must have time for yourself.

Wednesday 2nd
Today you should be putting yourself out there and ignoring
any emotional pulls to the past. There is a future calling you
to be your best self now. You may struggle to do this as you
are sensitive to reproach. Friendship groups will help to boost
your energy and offer support.

Thursday 3rd
Your ruler, Jupiter, may bring luck and benefits this year.
Listen to lessons about leadership, authority and expanding
your world this year. You may see that it's not just you who
is forging a new path. Your family are onboard, too. There is
more harmony in your social circle.

Friday 4th
Mercury turns direct today. Now you can look at your mission
with serious intent. You get a glimpse of your life purpose
today and this may fill you with optimism. Step up and take
charge of your own healing, and slowly look at the wounds
that are still open.

Saturday 5th

Today you may experience a conflict of interests between your own values and those of a group. You may need to retreat and see to things closer to home. This is good as it allows you to learn to prioritise, and your friends will understand. This angst will pass.

Sunday 6th

You may not be able to express yourself or get going on your projects today. This may be frustrating as you are keen to implement new changes and make space for something else. Social groups may be too demanding. Take time off to process how you feel. Are they in alignment with you?

Monday 7th

Today is a little easier as you are more inclined to ground your ideas and be more realistic. You may now have time to reconnect with social activities, including global concerns. You could have a startling realisation and a big need to communicate this to others.

Tuesday 8th

If you feel restricted again, it is because you have neglected a part of your psyche that is asking for healing. Maybe an old wound has reopened or an inner hurt has been triggered. Be true to your inner compass and realign with your own values today. Look at different perspectives to help.

Wednesday 9th

Today you are certain that you are heading in the right direction. There may be some indecision, which indicates that you are working through the pros and cons. Family can provide support and laughter, even light-hearted discussion, and their view can be useful to you. Listen to everyone now.

Thursday 10th

Your feelings are all about how far you can go and what is stopping you. You may wish to go further than you are ready for. Your sense of restriction may be an outdated coping mechanism, where you believe that you don't deserve to stretch your wings or swim to foreign shores.

Friday 11th

A good talk with yourself is needed now. Friends and social groups may offer a lot of advice, but you need to filter what you hear and decide if it is for you or not. Perhaps you have taken on something that is no longer serves your best interests.

Saturday 12th

The celestial lovers, Mars and Venus are getting close in your social circle. This heralds a time where you can integrate all sides of yourself to help the wider world and gain status. Logic, inspiration, desire and drive may be melded together to do something big soon.

Sunday 13th

Today you wish to stay close to home with a lover or a creative project. Romance is highlighted if you put your wider groups to one side. You have an opportunity to dream and be intuitive later today and this can be used for love or art.

Monday 14th

You may be grieving for something you have let go recently. This may cause you some heartache and you wonder whether you did the right thing. Your sensitive side feels this greatly. Try to be reasonable and think this through with logic. Have some quiet time to process this alone.

Tuesday 15th

Check in with your health today. You may not realise the effect that mental stress has on your body. Remember to put yourself first. If you need to express an opinion that may not go down too well, ensure that it is honest and kind. You may be compassionate and strong.

Wednesday 16th

Mars and Venus have met. You might step up as a warrior of love today. A full moon can put your duties and self-expression under the spotlight. You will certainly be making a stand today. Get ready for a few days with someone special who is more down-to-earth than you.

Thursday 17th

You may have forgotten about doing your personal inner work and something comes up that needs urgent attention. It's possible that you receive enlightenment and look at a problem in a new way. A partner may help to methodically work through this with you. Discussions are fruitful now.

Friday 18th

The Sun enters your sign today. Happy birthday! There is lovely energy for you to access and you may be fully aligned with a good cause that you are passionate about. A leadership role in this will suit you well. You are optimistic and looking forward to what the future brings.

Saturday 19th

You may be inclined to search deep inside your psyche for what needs healing. Some of it may be obvious, but be willing to look further for a root cause. Also, getting to know a special person on another level may be on the agenda for today.

Sunday 20th

A little setback may occur in your friendship circle and you put your group venture on hold. This is fine for now, as you have other things that need your attention. Remember that you have responsibilities to yourself too, and this may not be the time to ignore your own needs.

Monday 21st

Come back to your social and interest groups today as the energy suggests that great things can be achieved. You may find that you are networking far and wide, or on a mission to get to the bottom of something deep. Higher education courses may take up some of your time.

Tuesday 22nd

Conversations may be strained as you are not getting the information you want. However, you know you are following the right path and that what you seek is waiting around the corner. Be vigilant and get your groups to join you with this mission. Remember not to breach any personal boundaries.

Wednesday 23rd

You may be reviving a skillset you have learned in the past. Changes or endings need to be made and you may use old ways of doing this today. Your vision at work is wider and you may find that foreign travel is planned for this year.

Thursday 24th

Your mind may be working overtime today. Thought patterns and ideas may be surfacing to be filed for future use. Get your head down and attend to your work as this is no time for drifting into your own fantasy land. By the end of the day, you will have achieved much.

Friday 25th

Your inner compass is just out of sight, which is a sign that you must see to the daily grind instead. Watch out for illusions or things that seem too good to be true. Don't be easily led into a way of thinking that isn't practical or tangible.

Saturday 26th

This is a lovely day for getting together with friends and coming up with great new ideas. They may be radical, so do a risk assessment before implementing them. Philosophies make great conversation today and may show you a new way of thinking that you will enjoy discussing. Be open to new things.

Sunday 27th

If you can't get together with a lover, find your close friends who have shared interests, as today will inspire you to be the best version of yourself possible. You may have big ideas and begin to integrate new ideas into a plan of dedicated and passionate action.

Monday 28th

Be careful about what you express to others and how you express it. They may not be as flexible in their thinking as you and will need some time to come to terms with what you are saying. Your heart and head are in sync, and you are keen to put this into practice in some way today.

MARCH

· · · · · · · · · · · · · · · · · ·

Tuesday 1st

Today may be quite tiring so only do what is necessary.
Challenges arise that make you feel stuck. However, there will
be a breakthrough this evening. Go at your own pace and don't
get bullied into revealing more than you are ready to. You may
have a softer edge by bedtime.

Wednesday 2nd

A new moon in your own sign allows you to set goals that
pertain to your window on the world. This may be a new way
of thinking that enables you to see a different perspective and
act accordingly. You may be more optimistic once you have
worked this out.

Thursday 3rd

Big things can happen today from within your social sector,
which will impact your value system and passions. You may
now see a lot of things with great clarity and wish for a life
purpose that lifts you out from the mundane and into the eyes
of important people.

Friday 4th

Today would be a good time to check around your home
environment and look at what is holding you back. This
may be too many possessions or issues with money. What is
cluttering up your life? You may have the energy to declutter
or think up money-making schemes today.

Saturday 5th

The Sun meets Jupiter in your sign, which means that there is a lot of joy and good luck available to you today. If you need to showcase yourself and talents, now is an excellent time to do so. All your attributes combine well today to raise your status. You could be leading a group.

Sunday 6th

You can take what you have learned about using all your talents into your private life now. This reasoning coupled with compassion can ensure that you are in a good place to work hard on self-improvement and personal goals. Spend some time grounding and doing practical things, as well as time in your head and heart.

Monday 7th

You may come across as a genius today, and others will want to hear your ideas. Luck is on your side and this is a good opportunity to make a breakthrough in communications and plant seeds for something you wish to work on. Stick to the rules and you won't fail.

Tuesday 8th

An emotional pull towards your life purpose entices you to make small changes and tweaks in your lifestyle. Conversations may be enlightening but will give you too much to think about. This is a good evening for love, or a midweek family gathering may bring you support and encouragement.

Wednesday 9th

Your mind may be busy, so make sure you have space in your day to process things or share with another who can help. Home and family pursuits are favoured today as you drift between a need to expand and a need to dream. It's possible to find a happy medium.

Thursday 10th

Mercury enters your sign and you may notice how you become quite the chatterbox now. You may want to know the ins and outs of everything. Ideas will flow easily but you must remember to put them on paper and save them, as they may be of no use just yet.

Friday 11th

Let yourself be looked after today and give your body and mind a rest. If you have family members to see, prioritise them and then retreat and listen to your nesting instincts. Good food and company, people who you are on equal terms with or unconditional love from maternal figures will be good.

Saturday 12th

This is another lovely day for using your imagination to make things work. You may not need to go far to offer small solutions that can make big differences at home. Follow threads that you intuitively perceive as lucky chances that have been put in your way.

Sunday 13th

Your true north – your life purpose – is staring you right in the face today. It may become obvious what you are meant to be doing for this part of your life. You may need to switch something up for this to happen and may be unhappy about doing so.

Monday 14th

Today you may need to curb any excessive behaviour or reactions. It's possible that you come up against some tension that angers or upsets you. Your emotions could be on the edge, so tread carefully. Try not to take things too personally as they may not be aimed directly at you.

Tuesday 15th

The tension may continue today. The best thing you can do is to get on with your daily routines and keep a low profile. It may be hard to bite your tongue and say nothing, but things will run better if you do. Authority figures may call you in to account for yourself.

Wednesday 16th

Let a partner or someone close take some stress from you. Talking things out with them may help you to see and think in a more methodical and critical way. It's possible that you have been over-sensitive and misjudged a situation. Listen carefully to wise words today and be open-minded.

Thursday 17th

Put your dreams and visions to one side today and use logic and reason to solve a problem. You may find yourself having many conversations or messages to get to the bottom of something. Make sure you read all the manual and check all the details, and you will have a measure of success.

Friday 18th

A full moon in your opposite sign may show how you have been working on a relationship that now has a chance to shine brightly. You may have found a partner who can fill in the gaps you think you have. This can be a mutually respectful and unconditional relationship.

Saturday 19th

There is strong balancing energy available to you now. You may wish to search deeper into your psyche for very old wounds to heal. It's possible that you find something that shocks you, but now it has surfaced, you can do something about it and lessen its effect.

Sunday 20th

The spring equinox adds to the harmonising energy today. As you prepare to step into the longer, lighter days, pause and reflect on what you wish to take with you. Is there something you can leave behind? You may need to be ruthless about this and cut away harshly.

Monday 21st

Today may not feel very nice and you may be edgy and restless. It may feel as if your work is futile and not challenging. You may even have an overwhelming urge to get away, travel or take on a course of study. Conversations are unfulfilling today and may leave you dismayed.

Tuesday 22nd

This can be a big day of change as you begin to let go of what is weighing you down. Be careful that you don't antagonise the wrong people with your brutal attitude towards discarding what you no longer need. This may lead to some personal triggers being set off.

Wednesday 23rd

You have more than enough energy to make things happen today. This may involve your career goals, so put yourself forward and show how assertive and passionate you are. You may even be coercing someone to align with you by sweet-talking them. You are a slippery fish today.

Thursday 24th

Be very careful that you are not breaking any rules today. You may not understand that someone is not seeing what you see. Don't push their boundaries as you may be out of order. Watch what you say as it may be used against you in the future.

Friday 25th

If you can, show your innovative thinking in solid plans. It's possible that you can win someone around by showing hard evidence and not just quoting hearsay. It may grate on you that your words are not enough, but you will win points if you can be more practical and tangible.

Saturday 26th

Today it's imperative that you say what you mean and mean what you say. All eyes are on you. This is a crucial time where you may be in a make or break situation. Friends, associates and your interest groups are counting on you to bring radical but ethical changes now.

Sunday 27th

After all the excitement, the best thing you can do today is to take a break. Alone time will help to recharge your batteries for the next round. Whilst resting, you may have fresher ideas that will not be so difficult to implement and won't include having to persuade others.

Monday 28th

Be respectful at all times today. You may be jumpy and wish to get more points across, but you are being forced to wait. Your emotions spiral between anger, high energy, desire, compassion and responsibility. Love and obedience will win the day. You may feel spent and drained by bedtime.

Tuesday 29th

The best thing you can do today is to withdraw. Switch off and go back to being that dreamy, passive, imaginative, intuitive person. You may feel that you haven't been yourself recently and you would be right. Get ready to reconnect to your centre and find your life purpose once more.

Wednesday 30th

Solitude can bring you many blessings. You are returning to land whilst still connected to the imaginative world you love and excel in. You will benefit from a quiet mind today and if anything does pop up, you know to keep it filed for another time. Enjoy your peace.

Thursday 31st

What has changed for you? It may be an attitude, a perspective or something from within your friendship and social circle. You may feel a fresh new start coming, so feel your way into it before committing. Check out the lay of the land before drifting into it.

APRIL
······················

Friday 1st

Your head and heart could be working together to make set intentions under the new moon. Money-making schemes as well as plans for self-care and beautifying your home are favoured now. You may be emotionally invested in switching up your home environment for the better or minimising the clutter around you.

Saturday 2nd

This may be a busy day around the home as you implement your new moon goals. It may be difficult to let go of some baggage. You may also decline invitations from friends right now, while you spend time organising and restructuring. There will be time to socialise tomorrow.

Sunday 3rd

You may have had a sleepless night as your mind does overtime. This is your subconscious telling you what needs to go to make space for something of more value in your life. You may wake up with fresh energy to continue throwing out and giving yourself or your home a makeover.

Monday 4th

You may not be ready for the working week. The energy you have is more focused on cleaning up, clearing out and rooting around for things that are harming or hindering your growth. Conversations can be unhelpful as you may feel unwilling to listen and do your job properly.

Tuesday 5th

Friendships and interest group may give you a break from your powerhouse activities. Your family may also make suggestions that you welcome. Venus enters your sign to add harmony, beauty and more self-love. You may begin to learn how to fill your own cup first now, and this may unsettle others.

Wednesday 6th

A midweek get-together with family may prove to be beneficial as someone may have advice to share. Listen to the experience of others and think about taking onboard ideas you may not have previously considered. Laughter and playfulness within your family can lighten your serious mood.

Thursday 7th

If you can be more realistic and goal-orientated, you may learn that some dreams are possible, and others are simply a waste of your time. You may need to have a talk with your inner critic. Love and romance are highlighted for an evening of comfort, good food and security.

Friday 8th

Today there may be a little voice in your head urging you to do something, but you aren't quite sure what. By evening this will all be made clear and you should get the green light to say, plan or act. This may bring an old habit or situation to the surface to be cleansed.

Saturday 9th

If you desire to chase a dream with a lover or make beautiful art, today is the day. You are the mystic and poet of the zodiac, and you may find your muse now. You may wish to shout it from the rooftops or protect it. Choose wisely.

Sunday 10th

You may worry about having said the wrong thing too soon or completely misjudged a situation. Worry not, this is a passing phase and you are just being sensitive. If you remain uncertain, say nothing and keep a low profile; you may find that it's taken out of your hands.

Monday 11th

Conversations will be more serious now. They will have better foundations and fewer possibilities to be misunderstood. You have a chance to act on your dreams today as Jupiter and Neptune meet and shower you with blessings. Your ruler and true north are aligned so make that wish right now.

Tuesday 12th

Once again you are worrying if you have done the right thing. Relax, that voice in your head is your inner critic. Luck is still on your side so think big. You have an ocean of possibilities and a world of expansion coming your way. Jump right in.

Wednesday 13th

Today you might battle between doing something for you and pleasing a partner by going along with their wishes. Try the art of compromise without submitting and dismissing your own desires. You may give yourself a surprise by how well you are able to do this today. Be confident and assertive.

Thursday 14th

A struggle might occur with a partner or close friend today as your agendas clash. This isn't serious, but as you are a sensitive type you might feel it personally. You may wish to retreat and have some alone time. By evening you can both reconnect and restore harmony.

Friday 15th

You have four planets in your sign. You may feel vulnerable and exposed. Alternatively, you may feel strong and ready to swim to the furthest and deepest seas to achieve your dreams. Know that both these states are possible, and it's up to you how to react under stress.

Saturday 16th

A harmonising full moon will show you how far you are willing to go. You may not realise how deep you already are, and you are surviving this easily. Look around at who has supported you and take time out to give gratitude and credit to others where it's due.

Sunday 17th

Your energy is high, and you steam through the day. You may be following a secret passion or one that you are yet to understand fully. Long-distance travel, communication and exploration of other cultures may fill your day. Maybe you can arrange holiday time now and look forward to new adventures.

Monday 18th

There is unsettled planetary energy today. You may want to stick to the job in hand and distract your mind from wandering into unknown territory. The only thing that can stabilise you is connecting to your inner compass and not straying far from home. Get ready for a rollercoaster ride.

Tuesday 19th

You are not quite sure how to play today. Instinct tells you to get your head down and work, but you have an urge to do your own thing. Simply get through the day and wait until you are home to satisfy your own agenda. An exercise class will help.

Wednesday 20th

Communication is the key today. You must be very clear and precise, or you will be misunderstood and may be accused of being too unrealistic. Keep it real, especially when dealing with bosses, teachers or authority figures. Also, try to fix on something tangible to help ground you.

Thursday 21st

Plan ahead and schedule some time for friends or groups. You may find that folk with shared interests can offer you guidance and support. They may even fuel your resolution to be your best self. A leadership role in this area may give you new passion and unique possibilities.

Friday 22nd

This is a great day for exchanging information or research. Your mind will be busy assimilating new approaches to getting results. Use this lovely energy wisely and incorporate your own dreams and visions with the collective. This will benefit everyone involved and form a united front for much-needed change to occur.

Saturday 23rd

Good deeds and causes will take up much of your attention today. However, you may get frustrated if things aren't happening as quickly as you would like. Remember that this is not your personal agenda; it is shared by many and will need time to grow into something worth talking about.

Sunday 24th

Communications may hit a snag today. This will be temporary so try not to push things as they will soon be resolved. Turn to authority figures for guidance or look to others who have experienced this before and learn from them. They will be your best teachers at this time.

Monday 25th

Playing by the rules makes you feel better and you can slow down now. As the Moon drops into your sign, you may find that you are going with the flow more and enjoying it. You're aware that you're unable to push against the tide, so can relax a little.

Tuesday 26th

You are highly driven and passionate about your goals now. A commitment to a cause may have given you a new lease of life and taken your mind off unimportant situations that you tend to stress about. The rebel in you comes out and you are assertive in conversations.

Wednesday 27th

This lovely day has the best energy for you. You are probably in tune with what you are doing for yourself and groups. An agent of change is what you are becoming, and this will feature prominently on any future job or relationship prospects. Many blessings are being given to you.

Thursday 28th

What you say will make a huge difference in your friends and social groups today. It's possible that you are speaking up for a group and are raising your status as you do so. This doesn't matter much to you, as long as you are speaking sincerely and from the heart.

Friday 29th

Pluto turns retrograde today. A challenge may appear from out of nowhere, but as you have armed yourself with the necessary tools recently, you are able to deal with it well. This will be ongoing for some months. Ensure that you have done all you can for the moment.

Saturday 30th

A new moon and solar eclipse offers you a wildcard of a chance to set intentions regarding making things better in your environment. This may include raising your financial status. Venus and Jupiter meet in your sign, bringing lots of love, compassion, joy and empathy. Take this abundance you are being offered and make into something all can enjoy.

MAY

....

Sunday 1st

Spend time today putting finishing touches to something beautiful. You may be investing or spending on a large and frivolous purchase. Make sure you have the resources for it. It's possible that you shock yourself as you buy something on an impulse that you don't really need.

Monday 2nd

You may have some regrets today, but you talk yourself through the pros and cons and finally stop worrying. Your dreams may have prompted a little indulgence. Now it's time to enjoy it and use it as a starting point to give yourself what you deserve. Plan around what you can and can't afford.

Tuesday 3rd

There may be rows or disagreements today in the household as you find that you have to justify yourself in some way. Take care not that you neither become too aggressive nor let others walk all over you. Find it in yourself to take a stance that protects your own needs.

Wednesday 4th

Whatever change you experience today, it will be big. It may also be a very happy one and involve your community. Perhaps you have been responsible for this. You can easily rally the troops you need to stand beside you and start a revolution if you think one is necessary.

Thursday 5th

Unstable energy can be explosive today. This may present
in a positive manner and involve your social groups.
Communications can be volatile, too. However, this is also the
type of energy that makes huge differences when people come
together to fight for justice or a good cause.

Friday 6th

Your home needs your attention today. You may need to sort
out finances and balance your books. Family matters are
discussed, and you may succeed in bringing benefit to all.
Emotions are what drive you. You may be more protective of
your tribe and want to step up and defend them now.

Saturday 7th

Your ruler, Jupiter, spends his last few days in your sign for now.
If you need something, push harder. If you seek the truth, look
further. If it is joy and expansion you are after, step out, be seen and
learn to merge with the collective on a spiritual and ethical level.

Sunday 8th

You have the attitude of a spiritual warrior today. When
you combine compassion with action, you can become an
admirable leader and an inspiration to others. You may need to
have a hard conversation this evening, so be honest, assertive
and kind. Speak from the heart to get your voice heard.

Monday 9th

It may be tricky to manage all of your duties and remain
aligned to your passions today. Opposition may come from
your conditioned ways of reacting, and you may be forced to
face an old adversary. Stay strong and respectful. Don't be
intimidated or allow yourself to crumble under pressure.

Tuesday 10th

Mercury begins another retrograde cycle. Family issues and communications may come under fire. You may wish to spend time with a lover or person you admire now. They may be able to help you see through the fog you are experiencing in your head now. Mutual availability will strengthen bonds.

Wednesday 11th

Your plans and goals may get bigger, so take care that they are still attainable. Do they still hold value for you? Or are you making more work for yourself? You may be dreaming and acting without looking closely at all the details.

Thursday 12th

Little steps will be better for you today. Look at how to let things go, one by one. Keep checking the balance of what the benefits and hassles are. Think deeply and avoid making commitments right now. Mercury retrograde is asking for a pause or a redo in your family zone.

Friday 13th

Today you may notice that your community are all on the same page and moving forward together. There is a great uplifted feeling and you may see this more in your conversations and home life. Take care to check everything so you can be sure this is not an illusion.

Saturday 14th

There is a powerhouse of energy available to you at the moment. Love, compassion and harmony drive you to connect with other cultures and religions. You may simply watch documentaries or news articles. This may prompt you to learn more and discover the hidden mysteries of the world.

Sunday 15th

It's possible that you come up against a roadblock that restricts your need to explore today. However, this may be a sign to come back to your true north and look at your personal goals. Are they still right for you? Have they changed recently?

Monday 16th

A full moon and lunar eclipse may close a window of opportunity. You may notice this today in the workplace. Have you considered all your options? Remember not to sign anything just yet as this may still be an illusion. Wait until this energy settles.

Tuesday 17th

Relax today as the planetary energy is reasonably quiet. You may have time to contemplate your career advancement or think up a new money-making scheme. There are benefits to be had today, so keep your eyes open for anything you feel might help you personally. You may feel good about the year so far, and benefit from reflecting upon it.

Wednesday 18th

For a brief phase, you may feel as if you are swimming against the tide and being unrealistic. Talk to friends and associates as they may have a game plan or step-by-step process to help you achieve work goals. This may be arduous but is necessary.

Thursday 19th

Solid plans can be made if you talk to the right people today. You may feel that emotions are being pushed aside and you are unsure how to proceed. Sometimes you need to be more grounded, and today will show you how to tweak things without too much turmoil.

Friday 20th

You may be more positive today and feel as if you are back on track. Your community can support you in achieving the smallest of changes. This is a good start, as larger steps can leave you feeling overwhelmed. Listen to your self-talk this evening and dismiss the inner critic.

Saturday 21st

Be still, pause and take time out to reflect today. You may wish to do some introspection and think a lot of things through. Listen for messages coming from your dreams as they can guide you. Your mind is busy, and it may be hard to differentiate truth from self-deceit.

Sunday 22nd

A sense of duty drives you to make emotional decisions. Your conscience surfaces to steer you in the right direction. Try to mature your childhood conditioned habits and reactions. Ego wounds may resurface to worry you. This is the old you; leave it in the past and move on.

Monday 23rd

Communication may be tricky today, so stay out of other people's dramas and try not to create your own. There may be something you have overlooked that needs attention. A last-minute push may be needed to complete a project or prepare for an upcoming situation that will put you in the spotlight.

Tuesday 24th

It is crucial that you don't force a conversation or situation today, as you will come away from it badly. Instead, you have an opportunity to connect to your inner compass and dream away the day. Making a vision board by jotting down your thoughts can be useful.

Wednesday 25th

Your energy is high, and you are ready to act on your plans and intentions. You may be unrealistic so take a reality check with someone you trust. Make sure that what you have in mind is achievable and fair. Alternatively, you may be planning a home makeover and need advice.

Thursday 26th

An elder or voice from the past will be a good ally today. Your sense of duty to both your community and yourself allows you to make informed decisions. Your inner voice may be guiding you to act in a more mature and ethical way.

Friday 27th

You may be mulling over changes you need to make. These may be permanent endings or the start of a new phase of life. Your sensitive soul sees this as overwhelming. This is just a brief moment of self-doubt and it will pass. You may wake knowing which foundations to lay down.

Saturday 28th

You have a restless mind and heart today. However, this edginess can make great things happen. Think of the people you need to get onboard and how this will benefit you in the long term. You are about to get a financial boost from Venus.

Sunday 29th

Mars and Jupiter meet and together they show you where to put your energy for the best results. Look at what you value, and what you want more of. You have been given the green light to go out and get it now. Don't sign contracts or commit to anything just yet.

Monday 30th

A new moon and solar eclipse close the window on an event or situation within the family. It may also show you an ending of a research or educational project. It also allows you to set intentions, but as it's an eclipse you must be flexible and allow for adjustments.

Tuesday 31st

Today you may be concentrating on your work and using new skills and coping mechanisms. This is great as it shows personal growth. You may feel that this is not in your game plan but will soon realise that it's an important facet, and without it, you will drift away.

JUNE

Wednesday 1st

You may be in the mood for romance or beauty. A harmonising effect on your communication brings people to your side. Don't expect plans to take off today as you come up against blockages. It's likely that you just don't have the energy today.

Thursday 2nd

Expect love and surprises to go hand in hand today. You may learn something to your advantage. An overwhelming need to protect this information can make you feel rebellious or excited. Keep everything safely to yourself for now. You are privy to confidential knowledge that may be sabotaged if you share with others.

Friday 3rd

Mercury turns direct today and will relieve some of the pressure you may have had with communications within the family. Security is crucial now, so wait until you have been given permission before speaking out. There may be questions around control today, especially within friendship groups.

Saturday 4th

Saturn turns retrograde today. He is your greatest teacher. You may have a few months where digging around in your psyche seems harder than necessary. You may be going deeper and not like what you find. This only means that these are the issues you should consider healing at this time.

Sunday 5th

You may be feeling unsettled today. Anxieties may surface and cause you to run away from your responsibilities. It's possible that you have said something you shouldn't have, and being a sensitive soul, you are not looking forward to the inevitable confrontation. Stay calm and talk this through with trusted friends. Be ready to be accept responsibility for your mistakes.

Monday 6th

Reaching out to a partner may help to ground you and get you using logic and reason to work through a problem. Processing information on an emotional level will only make you more confused. Fact-checking and being methodical is the only approach available to you now. Support is there if you want it.

Tuesday 7th

Your ego may feel a little bruised today, but a partner will know how best to soothe you. Sweet words and sensual experiences may restore your calm. Conversations that are vibrant or radical can also pique your interest and get your mind wandering. Surround yourself with what you love.

Wednesday 8th

Whilst your imagination is doing overtime, you may notice that your rational mind is also making enquiries. A family issue that surfaced recently may be revisited and solved amicably. You may be putting a problem to one side or discarding it completely. You have checked the details and found that it isn't for you.

Thursday 9th

Be very careful with your energy levels today as it's possible that you do too much and become exhausted. You may be working through the night or being too much of a people pleaser. Look after your health, and duties will be easier to accomplish. Get rest if needed.

Friday 10th

Today may be very productive if you allow yourself to go with the flow. You may experience the first of Saturn's lessons today, so take note of any triggers that pop up as they are asking to be dealt with. Perhaps an issue with social groups or community needs to be addressed.

Saturday 11th

Take a rest day today and if you can, be alone with your thoughts. Self-care routines or exercise would be good. Conversations and chores may begin to be more stressful, so pace them well and schedule in time for you. Don't be tempted to act out of character.

Sunday 12th

A tricky day may test your patience. This energy can manifest in two ways for you. You may have volatile conversations with siblings. Or you may hold fast to your inner compass and ignore all advice. A fantasy island is what you want today.

Monday 13th

The working week begins, and you adapt nicely to your duties. There is a chance for expansion now. Look for a niche that needs exploring or a new direction for your career to follow. This will enhance your prospects so ensure that you step out of your comfort zone and stretch yourself.

Tuesday 14th

Today's full moon brings career issues to your attention. It's possible that you have achieved a qualification or received a bonus. There may be an opening or a completion of an existing project. Celebrate small achievements today without dumbing yourself down or making yourself small.

Wednesday 15th

Social groups may not be supportive today as you find some sort of injustice rotting away. This may be directed at you or you may have uncovered an indiscretion. If you speak out, make sure you have all the facts first. If you stay quiet, it will continue to bother you.

Thursday 16th

You may have a sudden urge to rebel and blow the whistle on underhand behaviour. There may be a conflict to deal with. This will trigger an uncomfortable feeling deep inside and you are unsure how to handle it. Let your defaults of empathy and compassion guide you.

Friday 17th

Take some downtime today as you may need to process recent events alone. Thinking things through may take you back to old habits and wounds. However, if you look at better ways of communicating and stand up for yourself, you will notice these wounds aren't as bad as you first thought.

Saturday 18th

Today may be challenging as you may be wallowing or dwelling on your own actions. You doubt that you have the ability to dive deep and heal. This phase will pass. Stay strong and give yourself a break. You are being hard on yourself. Get a new or different perspective.

Sunday 19th

Your mood lifts and you feel more like yourself. Venturing out will blow cobwebs away and fill your lungs with a sense of peace. You see your true north and realign with it now. Harmony within is important if you are trying to achieve the same in your outside world.

Monday 20th

What might you have overlooked regarding your home and family? Perhaps there is something that requires urgent attention. This may be a discussion or a family member you should check in with. You drum up the enthusiasm to chat about your dreams and visions with people who support you.

Tuesday 21st

The summer solstice arrives. The longest day gives you a chance to throw more light on your romantic and creative pursuits. You feel the change in the air and desire to get back on track about your passions. A feeling of optimism and the ability to be open can help.

Wednesday 22nd

Today you could be extra motivated or very tired. It's possible that you are making plans, writing lists or decluttering like a boss. An emotional pull to start new things may overtake you. Finish what you have already begun and refrain from making that to-do list longer.

Thursday 23rd

Siblings may be the medicine you need today. Phone calls, texts or visits may give you a boost as you revert back to childhood relationships when things were much simpler. Laughter and playfulness come with an enquiring mind. You may just want all the gossip as it takes you away from yourself for a while.

Friday 24th

If something is bubbling under the surface, pay attention to it. An uneasy feeling may rumble away until evening, when it'll burst out. A conversation might turn nasty so be careful. This is the same urge that makes you want to run away.

Saturday 25th

You may have noticed a lesson learned. Well done to you. Your inner compass is showing you a path that has twists and turns. Go with the flow and try not to resist any changes that are made along the way. These are all part of your personal growth and are beneficial.

Sunday 26th

Familial love can bring a happy day where everyone is on the same page and enjoying themselves. This is an optimistic day and you feel limitless. You may wish to expand your horizons or simply let others know that you are there for them. A carefree day can delight you.

Monday 27th

Your communications are like a hotline today. Your heart and head are in sync, and you may be researching, connecting or networking. You desire to know everything today. Be careful; you may push too far and cross a personal boundary or be triggered into old defensive habits.

Tuesday 28th

Neptune, your inner compass, turns retrograde today. You may begin to feel lost at sea. This period will activate a need to see different perspectives and perhaps dissolve any illusions you have been under. This will be uncomfortable at first, but as a Pisces, you will adapt easily to the new flow.

Wednesday 29th

A watery new moon offers you a chance to make goals and set intentions regarding your love-life and creativity. You may feel more sensitive now. An urge to protect loved ones becomes stronger and you may be at risk of smothering them. Give everyone a loving space and you will receive the same.

Thursday 30th

Power struggles may arise and test your patience. It may feel as if you are being denied the chance to grow, and expressing this will be difficult. You are probably thinking far too much of other's feelings and not admitting your own. Put yourself first today if you can.

JULY

·····················

Friday 1st

You are positively glowing today. Luck and love show up in the way you present yourself. Your health is good, and you may feel inner peace. People will stop and notice you now; you may not realise it, but you are turning heads today.

Saturday 2nd

Challenges may come from your family of origin and these may trigger an old hurt. You may be uncertain how to deal with this today, so why not give yourself time to think it through? A direct conflict between your needs and those of the family may upset the status quo.

Sunday 3rd

If a bad childhood memory surfaces, don't stuff it away and ignore it. Your inner child may be asking the mature you for advice. Think of the help you may have needed when young. What would you have liked to have been told? Can you heal a small part of you today?

Monday 4th

Today there may be an urgent need to make a plan, or you might find last-minute inspiration. You may have extra energy that comes rushing out of you now. Be careful as this can be draining. You may want to spend some time with a lover or partner this evening.

Tuesday 5th

You must watch what you say today. The rush of energy you have will also apply to words spoken, and something may slip out. You may hear gentle words of love that make you feel safe and secure. Sometimes happiness is forgetting your cares and letting another nurture you.

Wednesday 6th

Conversations may be misunderstood today. You may feel vulnerable for having shared too much. Perhaps you can retreat, or if someone is willing, you can explore your feelings with a logical, rational mindset. This isn't your usual stance, but will help you to gain clarity differently.

Thursday 7th

Care for your family is foremost in your mind. There may be an issue you manage well, and it changes your view of yourself. Boundaries need to be strong, yet porous enough to let others in. Keep it under your control. You are in charge of how much to let in and out.

Friday 8th

Today may be so intense that you use avoidance tactics to get by. This will hold off the pressure for a while, but you will need to deal with it at some point. Little things can dig at your conscience and demand attention, but your energy may be low.

Saturday 9th

A lover may be asking awkward questions. This is not to try and trip you up, but to get to know you on a deeper more personal level. If you're not ready for this, you may react like a small child having a tantrum. Let the mood pass and give each other some space.

Sunday 10th

You could have an urge to go out and explore. There may be a travel opportunity now. A day trip might suffice so make an impulsive decision and get out and about today. You will be surprised at how much you enjoy yourself. A group outing would be fun.

Monday 11th

A productive mood helps in the workplace, although it may wear you out if you choose to power through your tasks. You may need to look at your agenda and see where you can broaden it or follow routes that are unknown to you.

Tuesday 12th

Dreams may be strange or unsettling and this will flavour your day. You may wish to be more grounded and see to more down-to-earth chores. Emotions may still be lingering from your dreams or coming up from your deepest self. Deal with them another time; you must be practical today.

Wednesday 13th

There is a full moon today, which might show up something in your friendships and interest groups. It's possible that you have completed a mission and are now at the top and celebrating achievements. Alternatively, you may have reached the first milestone of a longer climb to success in your community.

Thursday 14th

Like a flipped switch, you notice a change in mood or motivation within a group. This may be at odds with what you desire for yourself. Alone time will help you to process your thoughts and evaluate a collective goal. Communicating this to others may be difficult.

Friday 15th

You may feel stuck today. The energy is challenging you to stay still and look before you take your next leap. An itchy restlessness will need to be tamed or channelled in another way. Self-control is important now and is one of Saturn's tests for you. Stay neutral if you can.

Saturday 16th

Subtle messages coming from your romantic and creative sides are asking you to listen. They may be uncomfortable or involve maternal figures you may have neglected. By evening, you may have the energy to reset the balance of give and take in your love life or within feminine relationships.

Sunday 17th

Your inner compass is also asking you to tune in and receive messages. If you feel the need to realign, then you must first find your centre of calm. Unusual conversations may intrigue you. Is there a family matter that requires urgent attention now? Are you the mediator or antagonist today?

Monday 18th

Venus moves into your love and creative activities. Now is the time for you to seek your muse. As the poet and mystic of the zodiac, you may find that you are more intuitive, sensitive and empathic than usual. Unfortunately, the need to get daily chores done gets in the way.

Tuesday 19th

Today it is important that you get something off your mind. You may have been putting off asking delicate questions or answering equally difficult ones. You are safe to enter this line of enquiry. Your childlike need to know how everything works will be satisfied. Go ahead and ask.

Wednesday 20th

Opening up or being inquisitive may have made you feel vulnerable. Take a look at what has triggered this. You may also be making changes at home, too fast and without thinking things through. Slow down today as you could be overwhelmed by evening. Be good to yourself.

Thursday 21st

A romantic rendezvous may get you excited. You have no need to fear, as this should be a very protective encounter, which may be passionate. Your conversations may seduce another and light a real spark, which, if tended properly may grow into a nice, slow-burning flame.

Friday 22nd

You get an emotional sense that someone has stirred up a longing within you. You may now feel connected to this person and would like them to share your dreams. Stay grounded now. You must learn about healthy attachments and personal boundaries. Take this slowly and keep it real.

Saturday 23rd

Your family are simply the best company this weekend.
You may be sharing responsibilities in an effort to lay down
foundations or beautify your home. All hands are on deck and
making a collective dream come true. Hard work comes with
fun and laughter today. Enjoy a family event or project.

Sunday 24th

You may be super busy making plans or putting yourself in the
spotlight now. You may notice that people are listening to you
or coming to you for advice. You have a huge heart and today
it is on show. The people around you are loving it, as are you.

Monday 25th

Romantic connections may have been put to one side as you
see to family matters. Today you may resume a connection
with a lover or someone special. You may not have time until
late, but when evening comes you slip nicely into a safe and
secure place of unconditional love.

Tuesday 26th

This is yet another day where romance is favoured. Your
heart's desires are right in front of you. Partake in what
delights these are, but be mindful that you are not selfish or
greedy. Remember that personal boundaries need to be healthy
and strong, and don't push too far.

Wednesday 27th

Surprises come your way today. You may see something in a new light, which may startle you, but in a nice way. You are likely inspired by a conversation or a person you have visited. This may prompt you to do something unusual and merge it with your personal goals.

Thursday 28th

If you wish to get something new off the ground, today provides the rocket fuel to do it. A new moon gives you the push. Set goals and intentions regarding health, creativity and speaking your truth. Your ruler Jupiter turns retrograde, so expect a lesson or two from him.

Friday 29th

Today you could have tests of patience in your daily duties. A roadblock or diversion puts you off track. You may also notice that financial matters and communications are also not straightforward. This is only a small hindrance, so bide your time and wait for the all-clear.

Saturday 30th

Today your head and heart are in sync, and you can get all your chores done with time spare for weekend fun. Watch out for a trigger that scratches an old wound. You may also be touching a sore spot on someone else. Partner time this evening can help you talk things through.

Sunday 31st

You may need to have alone time today if a partner can't help. You may be overthinking and getting yourself worked up. This energy may make you rebel or want to run away. This is avoidance. Whatever is niggling you needs to be given attention and healed.

AUGUST
·················

Monday 1st

Highly unstable energy propels you into the week. You may be more forceful in your communications and blaze a trail for your colleagues to follow. Your dynamic attitude may overlap into your love life as you possibly take giant steps to defend and protect romantic and creative projects.

Tuesday 2nd

A fiery mood may continue to make you more determined to lay solid foundations and tear away the old. It's possible that your directness unsettles someone who is unprepared for this. The energy is still heating up your love life, so expect surprises and unusual loving now. A new journey may be starting.

Wednesday 3rd

You are on a roll now, so keep the momentum going. Passion and desire can feel safe and secure. You may wish to express yourself in love much more than you have previously done. Messaging, allowing yourself to be vulnerable and placing new trust in someone special will benefit you.

Thursday 4th

Communicating with a partner or important person may help to negotiate deals and compromises. You may have more of an interest in other cultures or traditions at this time. Talk about this with knowledgeable people, and you may find yourself inspired to know more. Reach out to any friends overseas.

Friday 5th

A cry from the past might bother you today. This may be a health niggle that periodically returns. You may be frustrated or restricted in your movements. There may be an urge to rebel or give up on something. Hold on tight as this feeling will settle down soon.

Saturday 6th

Remembering your true north and purpose brings you back to fantasy thinking. It may be difficult to concentrate as you want more autonomy and feel the lack of it today. Jealousy may surface or another intense feeling threatens to overwhelm you. Friendship groups may offer the support you need right now.

Sunday 7th

Your dreams might be consuming you now, but you feel as if you are wasting time on them. The planetary retrogrades are the reason for this. You must spend time on your priorities before drifting around in your fantasy world. Shifts are not happening, and this may result in frustration or at worst, anger.

Monday 8th

Where did the weekend go? You're wondering where the time went, and may be feeling unproductive. Don't beat yourself up. Consider it essential time spent offline and in a different mode of thinking. This can be a healthy tool for relaxing.

Tuesday 9th

It's possible that you see control issues today. Issues around power between genders may appear in your social or interest groups or in your romance. This energy may mean that something you once thought beautiful, is now discarded. You may be giving up on an art project that no longer satisfies you.

Wednesday 10th

Today is a mixed bag of energy. Your wider groups will be the focus and may help you in several areas of life. Something in your love life may need addressing today before it gets forgotten about. Once this is dealt with, you can retreat and go into your inner world this evening.

Thursday 11th

You may feel uneasy as communications could be mixed up or misunderstood and emails may have gone astray or delivered late. This is likely no fault of yours, but you may bend towards that belief. As an empathic and sensitive soul, you may take on too many burdens today, so ensure that your voice is also heard among others.

Friday 12th

A full moon may bring parts of your psyche up for attention. This may be uncomfortable at first, but they need to be birthed into the present. You may notice how things have changed, or that your responses to them are not what they used to be. This is growth and development.

Saturday 13th

Be mindful that what you project out to the world matches what you are saying. Your walk must follow your talk now. Partners may be difficult to speak to, as your agendas are different. Don't worry as this is a passing phase that will blow over soon enough.

Sunday 14th

With the Moon in your sign, you may be more selfish or more typically you. It's possible that you dream the day away and have surreal conversations with friends. If this is what you choose to do today, go ahead. It will help you regain your sense of identity and self.

Monday 15th

Where in your life is there quality? Now is your chance to evaluate what holds value for you and what may be a waste of time and effort. If you want to switch things up, declutter and minimise your personal space. Today has the right energy to help you do so.

Tuesday 16th

Your mind may be ticking away, formulating new plans or a to-do list. You can surprise yourself and a significant other with your chosen topics today. A need for openness and the willingness to try different methods comes easily after a stubborn start. Check every detail for clarity.

Wednesday 17th

A defiant streak may appear today. Make sure that you have your say, but show restraint if it will make you seem selfish or needy. Go slowly with your work and only engage in conversations that have firm foundations and guidelines. You may have trouble finding harmony in some discussions.

Thursday 18th

Your inner genius may wish to come out, but you may have to wait and not rush into anything new. Take time to make sure that anything you began recently is complete first. Communicating with a lover may help you slow down and think.

Friday 19th

Reviewing your dreams and life path might assist you to make necessary changes. It might be that you must make more room, and this distresses you. Don't add to your workload. See what can be discarded without too much upheaval. Friends may not be helpful with this today.

Saturday 20th

You may be irritable and impatient this morning. As the day proceeds, your need to share information will increase. A family gathering can be active and fun, but do make sure that you are not the one doing all the work and putting in the most energy all the time. Aim for a collective effort.

Sunday 21st

If your dreams are not in line with others, don't despair. You are perfectly capable of a lone quest. You may feel disapproval from family members and lovers today, but this is your perception. Keep shining your divine self into the world and don't dumb yourself down for anyone.

Monday 22nd

A sense of love and protection fills you now, but this comes with vulnerability, too. This is a Pisces trait you know all too well. You may be willing to go the extra mile for someone else as this is natural to you, but avoid being the scapegoat or doing everyone's work.

Tuesday 23rd

The Sun now enters your partner area and will bring warmth
and health to your relationships. You may be brewing an
innovative idea or looking at unusual ways to communicate
with others. A short course of interest may be something you
would like to do in the near future.

Wednesday 24th

Uranus turns retrograde today. You may find that you have
a lot of breakthrough ideas that can be new or ingenious.
However, you may not trust them thoroughly and will need
to spend a long time researching their value. Power struggles
may leave a bad taste to your day.

Thursday 25th

If there is something you need to say to a partner and have
failed to do so, do it now. You may have a worry or concern
that needs clearing up. It's possible you have misunderstood an
intention and have been overthinking it. Get the facts straight.

Friday 26th

Anxiety rears its ugly head for a short while. You may feel
undervalued by elders or bosses. Restrictions and blockages
may also appear to be personal, but probably aren't. You are
just being sensitive to the atmosphere around you. Lie low
until you have processed this for yourself.

Saturday 27th

A new moon in your relationship area gives you the chance
to start again or set new goals to enhance your important
partnerships. Try not to discuss this just yet. Tricky energy
today means that you have to step carefully around others.
Harmony may be difficult to maintain.

Sunday 28th

If you have opened up to a lover, you may have unexpected repercussions. There is a line that is not for crossing at this moment, so protect your boundaries. The right time will come but for now, you must remain on your side and stay respectful and responsible for your actions.

Monday 29th

Your inner compass may seem lost to you today. However, your heart and mind are in sync so you can use this time to prepare and plan your vision board and map for when you have the next green light. Get energised and kitted up so you are ready.

Tuesday 30th

The world seems bigger now, but there may still be something preventing you from moving forward. This could be a financial dilemma, which you will need to deal with. There may be a way you can resolve this. Selling a skill or talent may be the way forward. What can you offer?

Wednesday 31st

Friendships may be antagonistic today, so you may need to retreat and leave them to it. You have no time for pettiness and should not be offering your services to those who are unworthy. This evening may bring intense feelings, maybe jealousy. You play detective and try to find out why.

SEPTEMBER
. . . .

Thursday 1st

You may have a whimsical day where you think about the past.
A nostalgic feeling comes over you and you may think about
college, university or holidays you have experienced. Will this
prompt you into booking more? Perhaps not, but you enjoy
reminiscing and it feeds your soul.

Friday 2nd

A longing may activate feelings of wanderlust, but you know
there is nothing you can do about them. Your personal journey
may be very different now. You know there are things you
can change in your community to make your world more
enjoyable. A collaborative effort with groups may bring about
those changes.

Saturday 3rd

You may be called upon to talk about what interests you.
However, this may be tricky as you appear to come up against
leaders or people with more knowledge than you. This may
make you feel insufficient and unimportant for a short while.
Your career is on your mind most of the day.

Sunday 4th

Think about where your skills can be put to more use. You
have a lot of love and passion to give and may now feel that it
is going in the wrong direction. A dilemma puts you between
work obligations, your dreams and mundane duties.

Monday 5th

Venus enters your relationship area today. She will help to bring more harmony and balance to your most important connections. Social groups may feel antagonistic and you may need to step up and become the peacemaker. Bring a little of that Piscean empathy to your community.

Tuesday 6th

This is a challenging but productive day. You seem to know exactly what to do and say to solve a long-standing problem. This may mean that you let something go or make a permanent change. Conversations can be difficult, but with respect and kindness, you may succeed in preventing a riot.

Wednesday 7th

You may want to spend some time alone to recharge your batteries. Staying in a place of peace will energise you. Your drive, mind and heart will be perfectly in sync, making you feel strong and maybe invincible. Inner work is easy now as you are open to changing your perspective.

Thursday 8th

There may be a lesson for you today, which could show how wide or narrow your personal boundaries are. If you overstep the mark with someone or they with you, this is your chance to evaluate how strong or malleable you are. This may be through conversations in which stubbornness occurs.

Friday 9th

As the Moon drops into your sign, you may feel vulnerable and exposed. You may not feel like loving yourself, and have feelings of unworthiness. A partner or friend may try to convince you of how wrong you are. Try to come out of self-pity mode and listen.

Saturday 10th

Mercury turns retrograde once more. You may be rethinking any connections you have made recently. Money and shared finances may be an issue now too. The full moon in your sign puts you in the spotlight and it may be uncomfortable if you have not been doing your inner work.

Sunday 11th

You will need to be careful of what you say today. The pressure has lifted, and you feel less vulnerable, but this may make you over-confident. Conflicts are likely, especially with leaders, bosses and teachers. Bite your tongue and save it for another day if you can.

Monday 12th

Today you have a better grasp of what requires your attention and efforts. You will be pleased with yourself if you can stick to the facts, tend to your duties and be respectful of personal boundaries. Your family may provide the fuel for your day and offer you support.

Tuesday 13th

Be determined and focused on the task in hand now. You may have a chance to up-level your status or be a prominent and proactive figure in your community and friendship groups. Slowly does it. Take one small step at a time and keep your eyes on the goal. Stay grounded and practical.

Wednesday 14th

Support from your important relationships will mean a lot today. You may be able to see into the future and make plans with others that are more attainable. It's possible that you have a breakthrough moment by evening, which may keep your mind busy into the night. Make sure it's worth the late hours.

Thursday 15th

Your dreams seem both far away and closer than ever. They may be illuminated in an unusual way. Social groups may have wisdom to share, which will benefit you personally. A transformation or a simple tweak in your vision may make the biggest changes for least effort.

Friday 16th

You may have a mishap today thanks to Mercury retrograde. If you can make sure that conversations are fully comprehended and both parties know what is expected, this may be avoided. Watch out for conflict between masculine and feminine energies. Travel plans also need to be double-checked today.

Saturday 17th

Emotionally you may be in turmoil. This will pass but until it does, ensure that you are keeping a distance from drama and tension that doesn't involve you. It may still upset you, but you need to remember that you can't solve everyone's problems just by being a sympathetic soul.

Sunday 18th

Your sensitivity may be the undoing of you today. You may be building towards a clash with someone in authority that will affect you deeply. This is avoidable if you slow down and protect what you cherish rather than going on the defensive too hard or too readily.

Monday 19th

Romance is highlighted as you wish to connect with someone who makes you feel safe and secure. This may also be a maternal figure with whom you would like to share familial love and traditional home-cooked meals. Feed your soul with music, poetry, love and romance. Feed your belly with your favourite food.

Tuesday 20th

If you feel a little smothered today, step back and give yourself space. Alternatively, you may revert to childhood conditioning and habits that have outgrown their usefulness. Look at your natural responses today and see if you can mature them in some way. Your inner child will be on show now.

Wednesday 21st

If you have something to showcase, you may be doing it now. However, take care not to blow your own trumpet too much, as it may backfire on you. Remember, Mercury loves communication but in retrograde he prefers you to go inward and think about things more.

Thursday 22nd

You have the right type of energy to make things happen today. You may be standing up for a good cause or showing an example to a younger member of the family. Be very careful about how you act as all eyes are on you today and you can't mess up.

Friday 23rd

It's very important that you open your mind and listen to any subtle messages today. Hints or advice concerning partnerships and intimacy may come your way to store and process later. An interesting day regarding how you conduct love affairs may be both emotional and intellectual. Be mindful of how you respond.

Saturday 24th

Your dreams with a partner may not be in sync today. You may feel slightly lost and find yourself wandering into unreasonable thinking. There's no need to take this personally as it won't last long enough to cause a big gap between you both. It's just a mismatch of moods.

Sunday 25th

Your emotions may threaten to overwhelm you as you feel unheard, unseen and not witnessed. A lot is going on for you that you are sensitive to. A new moon may be what is giving you unrest, but is also the chance to put things the way that brings most harmony.

Monday 26th

This morning you may wake knowing what needs to be changed in order to move on in your relationships. However, you may wish to express this, but Mercury is ready to mix it all up and it may not come out as you intended. Think twice today.

Tuesday 27th

You may prefer to lie low today. As much as you try, you fail to think clearly and are afraid to mess things up even further. Your best option today may be to put your attention towards family matters and simple everyday chores. Children and laughter can help you to relax.

Wednesday 28th

If you wish to risk it, you may be able to have intense conversations that will help to sort out an urgent problem. Love for yourself and knowing your worth is vitally important now. The deeper you go, the more easily you'll be understood. Superficial conversations are not relevant today.

Thursday 29th

Tension may be all around you, but if you are adaptable, you can swim your way around it and be a winner. All you need to do is remember to be kind, respectful and responsible in all you do. A transformation or a permanent ending may be the best result. New things will come of it.

Friday 30th

Putting your mind to something bigger than you will help now. Your search for the wider world and its mysteries may be achieved through the workplace. Take time to consider how your work and home balance may be adjusted for the time being, and lighten your load.

OCTOBER

Saturday 1st

Although you may want to reach out and broaden your horizons, your thoughts are too muddled today. It may be that you are doubting your ability to achieve a dream. Communication with a loved one may be tense, but you will have the opportunity to put that right very soon.

Sunday 2nd

Mercury turns direct today, but clarity may still be evading you. Take a day of rest and enjoy some pampering or connecting with old friends whom you trust. Small steps are necessary now, there is no need to put in much effort and drain your resources all at once.

Monday 3rd

The working week may begin with a smile and hope in your heart. You may be ready to shake off the weekend blues and get networking. Connections may give you something new to think about, which will become useful in time. Keep it on a low flame for now.

Tuesday 4th

Going inside yourself and pulling out old dreams may give you a fresh perspective and room to make your current ones happen. You may be torn between joining a good cause and deepening a bond with a partner. Either way, something may grow and expand today. Give it space.

Wednesday 5th

You may be faced with a challenge, which appears as a restriction. You may find a way around this or break through it by discussing it with family. Talking through the problem in your mind may give you too many options, so find an elder or authority figure to brainstorm with.

Thursday 6th

The Moon in your sign allows for a dreamy day. You may come across as idealistic but happy. Anything you are faced with today will be easily managed as you can be more adaptable now. Go with the flow and enjoy the freedom of movement you have today. It suits you well as a Pisces.

Friday 7th

Relationships could be your main focus now. You may notice subtle changes that make big differences and help your friendships and romantic connections move on. Conversations may be tricky but will produce the desired results in the end. Transforming the old into something new will always work if your communication is clear and precise.

Saturday 8th

You may be perfectly aligned with your true north today. A weekend activity doing something that falls into this will lift your spirits. However, you may find that you are so busy incorporating this that partner time is neglected. You may need to involve them and show them their worth.

Sunday 9th

There is full moon today, which may show you just what it is you value most. You may be inspired by more ideas than you can cope with. Pluto turns direct and change is inevitable but welcomed. Take care of yourself and your important relationships. Organise a Sunday treat.

Monday 10th

Your readiness to start the week with a bang is noticed by others. You may be more refreshed and prepared to tackle anything. Let partners know how much you appreciate them. Alternatively, have that conversation you have been putting off. After kickstarting the week, you may now settle down peacefully.

Tuesday 11th

Discussions deepen now. You may notice that you are more able to talk about issues that are difficult. You may want to know more about a partner as you can see them in your future. This may be the right time to approach the deeper mysteries that fascinate you.

Wednesday 12th

It's likely that you have an urge to break free from the norm today. There are some restrictions in place, and you must toe the line before doing your own thing. There will be time at the end of the day to dream, plan and rearrange your reality.

Thursday 13th

Family, especially siblings can be a source of entertainment for you today. You may find yourself in a leadership role you don't want but you agree to it. Research or critical thinking is a skill you need to draw on now as there are many interesting things you wish to learn.

Friday 14th

This is the perfect day to use your mental faculties to bring about more harmony, depth and responsibilities. You may find a solution to managing your time better. Family, relationships and alone time will all benefit today. Feminine energy and maternal figures will feature highly and may lead the way.

Saturday 15th

Your energy may be focused on family matters and your romantic pursuits over the weekend. You could be involved in a family gathering, which is nurturing and gives you an outlet for your creativity. This time should be used in a group effort to protect and cherish those you love.

Sunday 16th

Try not to jump in at the deep end or talk about subjects others may find awkward. You have the opportunity to revisit the past and look to the future, blending both nicely. Financial matters might arise especially concerning investments, shared accounts and legacies. These may be tricky to discuss.

Monday 17th

A rebellious streak might flavour your day. You may be putting your foot down and insisting on your own way. Control issues and power struggles may be a reason for you to retreat or defend things and people you care about. Keep an unbiased frame of mind if you can.

Tuesday 18th

Remember that duty comes first and play later. It's possible that you're being a little selfish today and wish to do your own thing. If you push against the status quo, it will push back, and you may find yourself in a tricky situation you will regret.

Wednesday 19th

Use your thought processes well today and they can bring you much-needed clarity. Love relationships are highlighted if both parties have the same agenda. You may find a partner in crime or a playmate who is truly on your side. Just take your time conquering the world together.

Thursday 20th

You are a warrior of the heart today. What you do today will be noted and likely commended. Put your best foot forward and show the compassionate, empathic soul you are. You may achieve a nice balance between masculine and feminine thinking and roles. You come across well to all.

Friday 21st

This is a pleasant day. You could be thinking about holidays or long-distance travel and connections. Planning a vacation for the future may be an enjoyable activity. You can look at past experiences and choose to revisit them or make plans for new, exotic adventures further afield.

Saturday 22nd

Partners may need a bit of coaxing to come onboard with a plan of yours. You sincerely want them to have a taste of something you enjoy. This may involve your wider friendships and interest groups. An earthy, practical activity such as a walk outdoors may be what is needed today.

Sunday 23rd

Are you ready to expand your horizons and deepen a love relationship even further? It may be that you have fallen in love with a religion or philosophy and may be spending a lot more time on it. Saturn turns direct and lifts some pressure from your self-reflection and inner work.

Monday 24th

Your mind and emotions are blended today meaning that you may be talking and discovering what makes you and a partner tick. There is an ease to today that brings harmony and balance to the most precarious of relationships. You may have learned more about boundaries from Saturn this year.

Tuesday 25th

A new moon and solar eclipse bring opportunities galore. This may be the green light you have been waiting for regarding longer holidays or connecting with a culture that is different from yours. Your heart may be reaching out and yearning for intense experiences that will broaden your mind.

Wednesday 26th

You may be reflecting on the past today and this may cause you some tension. You mustn't think about what you once valued and lost. This may make you feel miserable and will dampen your mood somewhat. This urge will soon pass, so try not to get stuck in negative thinking.

Thursday 27th

A lot seems to be opening for you now. You have just the right amount of energy needed to split time between family and love relationships. Combining the two may relieve some pressure. It's possible that you are stepping into the unknown at work.

Friday 28th

Your ruler, Jupiter returns to your sign. Now is the time to think about the leaders and teachers who have inspired your own path. You may find that it's you who has been an inspiration to others recently. Give gratitude where it's due to those who have helped form your life.

Saturday 29th

Be careful how you manage your time today as things may be moving too fast for you. It's possible that you tire easily and need more rest. Family can drain you so set limits on time spent here and make plans for a night out with friends this evening, which can be lively and fun.

Sunday 30th

You may be enjoying a seductive time in the early hours. Mars turns retrograde today. This happens in your family area and can mean that collaborative efforts are futile for now. You may notice more tension in this area too. Energy can be harder to find at these times.

Monday 31st

Detach from someone or something that may not have been good for you. This may be a habit, person or situation. Consider retreating and having some quality time to yourself for a while. There may be things surfacing from your psyche that are difficult to process and this will take time.

NOVEMBER

······················

Tuesday 1st

You may feel stuck or unable to proceed in any one specific direction today. This will feel particularly frustrating in your communications. This is a quickly passing phase, so don't wear yourself out trying to get results. Instead, use this time to evaluate the lessons of the year and reward yourself.

Wednesday 2nd

It's possible that you are thinking of lost loves or relationships from the past. Alternatively, you may be considering how you can look after yourself better. Long-distance connections may offer you something that appeals to your romantic and seductive sense of adventure. An exotic holiday or enticing retreat, perhaps?

Thursday 3rd

The planetary energy suggests that you can be fluid, dreamy and mysterious today. This may bring out deep and intense emotions. Follow where these lead as you may find a new self-care practice or spiritual path, which helps you grow and develop. Yoga or meditation would be the perfect activity today.

Friday 4th

Something may have stirred from deep within you. Look to your inner compass and you will see that you are right on target. You may not be full of energy, but you are inspired and determined to make the right sort of changes in your life. It's time to conquer the next ocean.

Saturday 5th

The little rebel in you might be choosing to do exactly what they want. This may ruffle a few feathers, but you are oblivious. Conversations may be narcissistic now and you may get into situations that threaten to disempower you. Be careful today.

Sunday 6th

You appear to be having blasts from the past frequently. They might come up in a conversation or a person you haven't connected with for a long time may message you. There may be secrecy or ulterior motives. Keep your wits about you.

Monday 7th

There may be another of Saturn's little tests for you today. Ensure that your personal boundaries are strong and healthy. You may find that someone is trying to barge their way uninvited into your life. Make your communications to them very clear and precise so there is no misunderstanding.

Tuesday 8th

A full moon and lunar eclipse occur, which may close a door on a recent difficult episode. You must be fully aware of everything going on today. It's possible that you uncover a secret or hear gossip now. Say nothing for now, but listen well.

Wednesday 9th

The energy is building to a potentially volatile outburst. Exposure is possible. This may be you or someone else with whom you have been in contact a lot recently. Practise stepping away from other people's dramas and kindly cut them off if you think it would be best.

Thursday 10th

You may have trouble with responsibility today. Perhaps you need an ally who can keep you strong and secure. You may be at risk of being swept away with the emotional current, so keep one foot on the ground. Take off your rose-tinted glasses and see a situation for what it really is.

Friday 11th

It's likely that you feel drained today. You may have lost your faith in some friends or family members and need to be alone. If you have private time, make sure you're not wallowing in self-pity. Use the time constructively or create art.

Saturday 12th

Romance can be a welcome distraction. There is enough watery energy around for you to feel perfectly at home protected by a lover. You may also be in the mood for music, poetry or art. This is a perfect day for self-expression. Stay in a safety bubble and create something beautiful.

Sunday 13th

You may notice the benefit of expressing your emotions now. Small changes, surprises and breakthroughs can make dreams come true. You can manipulate your own reality and realign with your true north. As a Pisces, you'll thoroughly enjoy swimming in today's ocean. Where might you drift off to?

Monday 14th

If you happen to be floating or swimming on this helpful tide, who would you like for company? A spiritual teacher may make themselves available to you. Use this time to merge with fellow travellers and connect with your divine self. You may be on show this afternoon.

Tuesday 15th

You may have a feeling that something is being taken from you. Stay calm, as this isn't quite what is happening. You are being asked to make a final effort to go after your desires concerning travel, philosophy and religion. Plan that holiday now. A phone call may put you on edge this evening.

Wednesday 16th

Do only what is necessary today. You may feel your energy slipping away or your focus being shifted elsewhere. This is a natural effect of two planets shifting signs together. You may notice this more in the workplace, so keep aware of things that you should know.

Thursday 17th

Partner time can help to soothe your mind, which may be in a muddle right now. Those closest to you might know how to sift through the facts and check every detail, whereas you might feel too emotional to think rationally. Prepare for the workplace to occupy most of your thoughts now.

Friday 18th

You may still experience some confusion. This is the shift from intense inward focus to one that is expansive and needs you to be dynamic and outgoing. You may feel irritated with family members today, as they need your attention and you are not in the frame of mind for them. Be patient with them.

Saturday 19th

Today may be exhausting as you may have no time for yourself. Tension may lead to rows within the family. By evening your mood may lift, enabling you to get to grips with a new role or target at work. You may need to broaden your thinking.

Sunday 20th

You can step up to your responsibilities today, which helps take your mind off troublesome overthinking. A sense of equilibrium returns and this can help you to enjoy the remainder of the weekend. Work and play come in equal measure today. Say no to anything that tips the balance.

Monday 21st

Your busy mind returns to foreign lands and other cultures. Watching documentaries or doing a little research may satisfy that urge to explore. It's possible that you are working towards a new opportunity at work, which will be inspirational and raise your status. Go with the flow and keep afloat.

Tuesday 22nd

You may drift back into whimsical thinking today. Deep and intense feelings may surface, and you may need alone time to process them. The Sun moves into your career area, as if to confirm that there is something bright and optimistic waiting for you just over the horizon. What can this be?

Wednesday 23rd

Your innermost thoughts may be keeping you awake, so listen to them. You may experience triggers that are simply asking you to find your edge and go there. In order to make a dream happen, you may have to meet it halfway and start the ball rolling from your end.

Thursday 24th

There is a huge green light right there in your career area.
A new moon and your ruler, Jupiter, turning direct are exactly
what you need today. This may be a huge career or travel
opportunity. You need to grab this with both hands and not
let it go if you are to make the most of it.

Friday 25th

Show others that you are worthy of what is to come. You may
be doubting yourself and wonder if this is right for you. Talk to
someone who has more experience and listen to their advice.
If you wish to climb the corporate ladder, you are already on
your way up the rungs.

Saturday 26th

Take a day to rest and recharge. Pause and reflect on the year
and congratulate yourself for your successes. There are more
than you realise. You may be looking back at past efforts and
smiling at how they have benefited you. Look to the future and
visualise yourself there.

Sunday 27th

If you need to tweak something or make changes in your wider
circle, you can do this today. You have luck on your side and
vision in your heart. Friends and interest groups can give you
their collective wisdom. Share from your side too and see how
enthusiasm can be infectious.

Monday 28th

Don't start the week on a downer. You have what it takes, and
it has been noted. You may feel blocked in some way, but this
is probably your own doing. Do something that lifts your self-
esteem and boosts your confidence. Look for inner strength.

Tuesday 29th

Searching your psyche may bring up the resources you need to make you believe in yourself. Think about times in the past where you doubted your ability but still managed to succeed. An elder or boss might offer you more support. Important conversations can wait until you have more information.

Wednesday 30th

The Moon drops into your sign today and you can relax. You may notice that you don't have to put in the extra effort to be witnessed, because people are already noticing your worth. You are the ideal person for the job, so stop listening to your inner critic and step into your power.

DECEMBER

. . . .

Thursday 1st

Conflicts between masculine and feminine energies are likely today. You might experience this in the workplace. This may make you extra sensitive as you are caught between two parties that are dear to you. Holding on to your inner compass may save the day, so stay true to your own values.

Friday 2nd

Your sense of justice and equality is strong today. You may wake to know that respect and responsibility are vital to solving any problems that occur. Try not to get too fired up before knowing all the facts. Getting what you desire isn't achieved by rushing into the unknown.

Saturday 3rd

Today is much more balanced as you find that you have empathy for those in trouble. This will do you good and bring you inner peace. You may need to lead the way or be seen as an example of what makes a team great. Treading slowly and gently helps.

Sunday 4th

Neptune turns direct today. You now have greater clarity about your spiritual path or personal ethics. However, a glitch in the day may knock you from your place of peace. Make this a day of short visits and catching up with those who matter to you.

Monday 5th

It's possible that you get a stroke of luck today, which can propel you forward on your path. Conversations may be the trigger for this. Listen carefully with an open mind, but again, don't rush into anything just yet. You may have an emotional pull to break free of restrictions.

Tuesday 6th

Elders in the family or authority figures may give you some problems today. You have a knack for keeping the peace, so this is no big deal. Allow yourself to keep a tight hold on your dreams and passions and be ready to make a last-minute push to impress the boss.

Wednesday 7th

Today may seem too quiet and that arouses your suspicions. There is no need to fret as this is simply a day where nothing much happens. A midweek family gathering where you can be childlike and unfiltered may be the exact remedy you need. Make time to enjoy a laugh with your tribe.

Thursday 8th

You may see a completion of a collaborative project in your family area. The full moon spotlights your communication, but beware, Mars is close and may induce tension. As always, you can use your gentle persuasiveness to restore harmony quickly. Celebrate successes and ignore petty squabbles.

Friday 9th

There is tricky energy surrounding your family today. You may find that gossip is rife, or people change their minds after an agreement. You may simply have to retreat and let it all die down. Stay safe and protected whilst keeping out of dramas that don't involve you. If they do, be respectful.

Saturday 10th

Friendship groups may be a welcome distraction now. The party season may have already begun, and you could well be filling in your planner. Something unexpected may cheer you up today. This may come in the form of a conversation or message. Responding with affection and curiosity will enhance your day greatly.

Sunday 11th

If you are in need of some fun and laughter, use the remainder of the weekend to think big, dream bigger and let everyone know about your vision. You may feel a little vulnerable doing so, but if you stay true to your soul and speak up, people will join in your enthusiasm.

Monday 12th

The week may begin with you feeling more outgoing and optimistic. You may have a passion for life today and wish to spread that around you. A challenge may present itself this evening. This may be a choice to reconnect with old friends or make new ones.

Tuesday 13th

Something is blocking your way today. This is temporary so don't worry. You may be struggling with an issue from the past or words that have triggered an old wound. Let it wash over you and you will realise that this is part of the healing process.

Wednesday 14th

You may wish to receive affection from a partner who can always talk you out of a low mood. It's possible that you are doubting yourself and thinking your dreams are unattainable. Your wider friendship groups are supportive and may take you out on a midweek get-together.

Thursday 15th

Have you noticed that you are far more grounded today? This is unusual energy for you as a water sign, but make the most of it. You may find that you slow down or choose one path over many. Alternatively, you may feel stuck instead of your normal fluid nature. Pausing isn't stopping.

Friday 16th

It may feel like you have lost sight of your inner compass again. This is because you are being asked to consider other things today, such as friendships, interest groups and social media contacts. You may be reaching out, or someone to you. A good cause needs your input.

Saturday 17th

Socialising may not be on your agenda today. This is fine; you are allowed to switch off and have alone time. You may have an underlying feeling that keeps you from connecting with friends. What is brewing for you? Is it just a tremor or a potential eruption?

Sunday 18th

Stay out of possibly manipulative situations today. Your heart and head aren't in sync, and this may cause you to make poor decisions. Act in a mature manner and be respectful at all times. By evening you may find that this tension has passed, and you can think more clearly.

Monday 19th

Although you may be left with a feeling of mistrust, your friendship groups may provide a source of lively communications. You may be thinking of travelling with a close friend or partner. This may also be a new adventure where you combine work with pleasure. Charities may get your attention now.

Tuesday 20th

Your ruler, Jupiter, leaves your sign today. You will now feel his jubilant, luck-bringing influence in your finances. This is exciting news and may enable you to finance your personal mission in the coming year. Watch out for people who push too far or demand too much from you today.

Wednesday 21st

Today is the winter solstice. The shortest day is the perfect opportunity to host a gathering of friends and reflect on the year. You may get lucky at work and catch the eye of someone influential. Colleagues may suggest a celebration in readiness for the festive season.

Thursday 22nd

Your energy can be low today, but you may still be able to enjoy a few surprises with friends. An invitation may come from someone you have not seen for some time. It may be difficult to commit to a meeting, but a phone call or messages may be enough for an enjoyable reconnection.

Friday 23rd

Get ready to party. A new moon is the start of the festivities and heralds a new shift in your friendships. You may be looking at joining new groups next year. Volunteering or taking a leadership role within an interest group may be a new calling and result in a rise in status.

Saturday 24th

This is a great day for socialising, communicating and generally having a good time. You may be celebrating in style this evening. Luxury dining and good conversation kick off a very special day. You may feel more at peace today and in love with everyone around you.

Sunday 25th

You may feel the broader effects of this day as your sensitive soul is on alert. The empathy you have for your closest friends and family is limitless, and your self-control enables you to be the perfect host. You may be the star of the show as you give equal attention to all.

Monday 26th

It's possible that you feel a little deflated today, but this is only natural. Everyone may be tired, and conversations are far more quiet. You may also notice that you need to refill your own cup as you have given so much from it recently. Do your duties as you need to, then relax.

Tuesday 27th

The Moon returns to your sign and picks your spirits up. The fun and games may still be going on and you have the right amount of energy to join in. Going with the flow may relieve any pressure you have around who to spend time with.

Wednesday 28th

Once more you may feel more tired than usual. Go easy on yourself today or allow for a few treats. Friends and your inner compass combine to make you certain you are on the right path. You may feel supported and encouraged by your colleagues and interest groups. Take a leap of faith.

Thursday 29th

Mercury turns retrograde today. Be careful with all travel arrangements and back up your devices. People may say more than they mean right now. They may also be prone to gossip or expressing love more readily than they intend. Keep yourself safe and slow down.

Friday 30th

It's possible that you have trouble staying still, but also have problems making any kind of progress. Family matters may be strained or exhausted. A low profile might help you to stay out of troublesome dynamics and recharge, ready to party tomorrow night. Don't push any complicated issues.

Saturday 31st

You are in the mood to celebrate; however, you may see some conflicts and problems with others. You may be the mediator in this situation. This could be a challenging evening but with a lot of self-control, you may come out of it the winner and be the one who restores harmony.

Pisces

· · · · · · · · · · · · · · ·

PEOPLE WHO SHARE
YOUR SIGN

PEOPLE WHO SHARE YOUR SIGN

. . . .

No pinch can take the faraway sign of Pisces out of their dreamland. With their artistic flair, compassionate hearts, and wonderful imaginations, Pisceans can both inspire and heal. Whether it's sharing their visionary talents like Alexander McQueen and Jenny Packham, or emotional lyrics like Kurt Cobain and Johnny Cash, the gifts from Pisceans can help restore a magic to the world. Discover which of these enchanting Pisceans share your exact birthday and see if you can spot the similarities.

20th February

Rihanna (1988), Miles Teller (1987), Trevor Noah (1984), Chelsea Peretti (1978), Kurt Cobain (1967), Cindy Crawford (1966), Walter Becker (1950), Ivana Trump (1949), Mitch McConnell (1942)

21st February

Sophie Turner (1996), Riyad Mahrez (1991), Ashley Greene (1987), Elliot Page (1987), Mélanie Laurent (1983), Jennifer Love Hewitt (1979), Jordan Peele (1979), Michael McIntyre (1976), Kelsey Grammar (1955), Alan Rickman (1946), Nina Simone (1933), Hubert de Givenchy (1927)

22nd February

Drew Barrymore (1975), James Blunt (1974), Chris Moyles (1974), Jeri Ryan (1968), Steve Irwin (1962), Kyle MacLachlan (1959), Julie Walters (1950), Niki Lauda (1949), Robert Kardashian (1944), Bruce Forsyth (1928)

23rd February

Dakota Fanning (1994), Skylar Grey (1986), Andre Ward (1984), Aziz Ansari (1983), Emily Blunt (1983), Josh Gad (1981), Kelly Macdonald (1976), Daymond John (1969), Kristin Davis (1965), W. E. B. Du Bois (1868)

24th February

Earl Sweatshirt (1994), O'Shea Jackson Jr. (1991), Priscilla Chan (1985), Floyd Mayweather (1977), Bonnie Somerville (1974), Billy Zane (1966), Steve Jobs (1955), Phil Knight (1938)

25th February

Eugenie Bouchard (1994), Rashida Jones (1976), Chelsea Handler (1975), Sean Astin (1971), Téa Leoni (1966), George Harrison (1943), Anthony Burgess (1917), Pierre-Auguste Renoir (1841)

26th February

CL (1991), Charley Webb (1988), Teresa Palmer (1986), Erykah Badu (1971), Max Martin (1971), Michael Bolton (1953), Johnny Cash (1932), William Cody (1846), Victor Hugo (1802), Christopher Marlowe (1564)

27th February

Lindsey Morgan (1990), JWoww (1986), Kate Mara (1983), Josh Groban (1981), Chelsea Clinton (1980), Peter Andre (1973), Li Bingbing (1973), Derren Brown (1971), Timothy Spall (1957), Elizabeth Taylor (1932), John Steinbeck (1902)

28th February

Sarah Bolger (1991), Olivia Palermo (1986), Karolína Kurková (1984), Natalia Vodianova (1982), Ali Larter (1976), Amanda Abbington (1974), Ainsley Harriott (1957), Paul Krugman (1953), Bernadette Peters (1948), Frank Gehry (1929)

29th February

Jessie T. Usher (1992), Mark Foster (1984), Ja Rule (1976), Pedro Sánchez, Spanish Prime Minister (1972), Tony Robbins (1960), Dennis Farina (1944)

1st March

Justin Bieber (1994), Kesha (1987), Lupita Nyong'o (1983), Jensen Ackles (1978), Javier Bardem (1969), Paul Hollywood (1966), Zack Snyder (1966), Ron Howard (1954), Harry Belafonte (1927), Frédéric Chopin (1810)

2nd March

Becky G (1997), Nathalie Emmanuel (1989), Bryce Dallas Howard (1981), Rebel Wilson (1980), Chris Martin (1977), Alexander Armstrong (1970), Daniel Craig (1968), Jon Bon Jovi (1962), Karen Carpenter (1950), Lou Reed (1942), Dr. Theodor Seuss (1904)

3rd March

Camila Cabello (1997), Jessica Biel (1982), Ronan Keating (1977), Alison King (1973), Julie Bowen (1970), Ira Glass (1959), Miranda Richardson (1958), Zico (1953), Alexander Graham Bell (1847)

4th March

Brooklyn Beckham (1999), Bobbi Kristina Brown (1993), Draymond Green (1990), Whitney Port (1985), Chaz Bono (1969), Patsy Kensit (1968), Sam Taylor-Johnson (1967), Tim Vine (1967), Khaled Hosseini (1965), Patricia Heaton (1958), Catherine O'Hara (1954), Shakin' Stevens (1948)

5th March

Madison Beer (1999), Taylor Hill (1996), Sterling Knight (1989), Dan Carter (1982), Hanna Alström (1981), Jolene Blalock (1975), Eva Mendes (1974), John Frusciante (1970), Lisa Robin Kelly (1970), Joel Osteen (1963), Talia Balsam (1959), Esther Hicks (1948)

6th March

Tyler, The Creator (1991), Agnieszka Radwańska (1989), Shaquille O'Neal (1972), Connie Britton (1967), Rob Reiner (1947), David Gilmour (1946), Valentina Tereshkova (1937), Gabriel García Márquez (1927), Michelangelo (1475)

7th March

Laura Prepon (1980), Jenna Fischer (1974), Matthew Vaughn (1971), Rachel Weisz (1970), Wanda Sykes (1964), E. L. James (1963), Bryan Cranston (1956), Piet Mondrian (1872)

8th March

Stephanie Davis (1993), Petra Kvitová (1990), Kat Von D (1982), James Van Der Beek (1977), Freddie Prinze Jr. (1976), Florentino Pérez, (1947), Randy Meisner (1946)

9th March

YG (1990), Bow Wow (1987), Brittany Snow (1986), Matthew Gray Gubler (1980), Oscar Isaac (1979), Juliette Binoche (1964), Bobby Fischer (1943), Yuri Gagarin (1934)

10th March

Emily Osment (1992), Ivan Rakitic (1988), Olivia Wilde (1984), Carrie Underwood (1983), Samuel Eto'o (1981), Robin Thicke (1977), Timbaland (1972), Jon Hamm (1971), Sharon Stone (1958), Chuck Norris (1940)

11th March

Thora Birch (1982), LeToya Luckett (1981), Benji Madden (1979), Joel Madden (1979), Didier Drogba (1978), Johnny Knoxville (1971), Terrence Howard (1969), John Barrowman (1967), Jenny Packham (1965), Alex Kingston (1963)

12th March

Christina Grimmie (1994), Stromae (1985), Jaimie Alexander (1984), Pete Doherty (1979), Aaron Eckhart (1968), James Taylor (1948), Liza Minnelli (1946), Jack Kerouac (1922)

13th March

Jordyn Jones (2000), Mikaela Shiffrin (1995), Kaya Scodelario (1992), Tristan Thompson (1991), Common (1972), Jorge Sampaoli (1960), Dana Delany (1956), William H. Macy (1950)

14th March

Simone Biles (1997), Ansel Elgort (1994), Stephen Curry (1988), Jamie Bell (1986), Taylor Hanson (1983), Chris Klein (1979), Brian Quinn (1976), Megan Follows (1968), Billy Crystal (1948), Michael Caine (1933), Quincy Jones (1933), Albert Einstein (1879)

15th March

Paul Pogba (1993), Lil Dicky (1988), Jai Courtney (1986), Kellan Lutz (1985), Eva Longoria (1975), will.i.am (1975), Bret Michaels (1963), Fabio Lanzoni (1959), Mike Love (1941), Ruth Bader Ginsburg (1933), Gerda Wegener (1886)

16th March

Wolfgang Van Halen (1991), Theo Walcott (1989), Jhené Aiko (1988), Alexandra Daddario (1986), Danny Brown (1981), Brooke Burns (1978), Sophie Hunter (1978), Alan Tudyk (1971), Lauren Graham (1967), Flavor Flav (1959), Victor Garber (1949), Jerry Lewis (1926)

17th March

John Boyega (1992), Hozier (1990), Grimes (1988), Rob Kardashian (1987), Edin Džeko (1986), Coco Austin (1979), Brittany Daniel (1976), Alexander McQueen (1969), Billy Corgan (1967), Rob Lowe (1964), Gary Sinise (1955), Kurt Russell (1951), Pattie Boyd (1944), Nat King Cole (1919)

18th March

Lily Collins (1989), Danneel Ackles (1979), Adam Levine (1979), Alex Jones (1977), Emma Willis (1976), Queen Latifah (1970), Peter Jones (1966), Vanessa Williams (1963), Grover Cleveland, U.S. President (1837)

19th March

Héctor Bellerín (1995), Garrett Clayton (1991), AJ Lee (1987), Bianca Balti (1984), Eduardo Saverin (1982), Kolo Touré (1981), Bruce Willis (1955), Glenn Close (1947), Ursula Andress (1936), David Livingstone (1813)

20th March

Marcos Rojo (1990), Ruby Rose (1986), iJustine (1984), Fernando Torres (1984), Freema Agyeman (1979), Chester Bennington (1976), Michael Rapaport (1970), Kathy Ireland (1963), David Thewlis (1963), Holly Hunter (1958), Spike Lee (1957), Douglas Tompkins (1943), Fred Rogers (1928), B. F. Skinner (1904)